NEVER GIVE UP
AND LIVE THE LIFE
OF YOUR DREAMS

From Fear to Love

Dear Brandon

Life is such a beautiful
adventure filled
with Love
Keep shining
your light
live your dreams
with Love
Sev

SEV JOY JAUNASSE

Quantity sales special discounts are available on quantity purchases by corporations, associations, and others. For details, contact the publisher at the address above.

Orders by U.S. trade bookstores and wholesalers. Email info@BeyondPublishing. net

The Beyond Publishing Speakers Bureau can bring authors to your live event. For more information or to book an event contact the Beyond Publishing Speakers Bureau speak@BeyondPublishing.net

The Author can be reached directly at BeyondPublishing.net

Manufactured and printed in the United States of America distributed globally by BeyondPublishing.net

New York | Los Angeles | London | Sydney

ISBN Hardcover: 978-1-63792-063-3

ISBN Softcover: 978-1-637921-08-1

I dedicate this story to my brother, Jacek, who is a pure miracle of life.

Your love of life and your smile remind me every day of the power of the present moment. I love you.

I dedicate this book to my children, Kelyan and Lea, who are my daily source of unconditional love. I thank you for being my teachers and remind me what I hold dearest in the world. I love you.

Finally, I dedicate this book to all women in the world searching for peace of mind and more meaning in their daily life. May the spark of love awaken your soul. You are a source of greatness and such an inspiration for tomorrow's generations, if you just allow yourself to believe in your worth. Reignite the child's spark in your heart today, and never stop believing in your greatest dreams.

Life is just about moments; cherish them all with all ups and down. We all have just one life to live fully; don't spend so much time on what is missing or what failed yesterday. Instead, appreciate what you have still today to be grateful for, especially in this challenging moment.

Be your best each and every day. Don't try to be perfect; it's a journey of little steps at a time; it's a journey of self-discovery. It's just about progress. Live it and share it authentically. We came here just for love and expansion of peace, and all that starts within us.

WHAT OTHERS ARE SAYING

I met Sev Jaunasse, several years ago, during a Tony Robbins event. I remember vividly the light that shone through her very being. It was beautiful to behold. I felt an instant connection with my new friend. It was a soul connection—pure and easy—like a gentle rolling stream.

Sev and I quickly discovered that we had both been orphaned as children, and that we were on a journey of healing the wounds of abandonment that happened so long ago. What we also shared in common was a belief that we could become more than the broken pieces of our story. That somehow there was miracle to be found within the messiness of life if we were willing to feel what needed to be felt in order to reframe our earliest experiences.

Key to the reframing were two important lessons:
1. Everything in life happens for us and not to us.
2. Our value is not determined by our circumstance.

Never Give Up weaves these essential lessons within its pages as it sets a framework for healing and deeper self-awareness. Sev shares her powerful story of a little girl in Poland who, against all odds, believed that the dreams in her heart could be realized, and that there is a big and beautiful life awaiting us beyond the fear.

Sev's words will awaken you to the desires of your heart as you begin to own your truth and emerge into the fullest expression of who you're here to be.

I'm grateful that Sev never gave up. She has dedicated her life's work to being the messenger of this truth: you are worthy of an exceptional life. Let her book fill you up and encourage you to pioneer your way to new frontiers of hope and healing.

Never Give Up will be your guide as you discover the miracles that await you when you open your heart to love and embrace the transformational power of now.

Michelle Madrid-Branch
Author, Speaker, International Adoptee, & Life Coach for Women
https://michellemadridbranch.com

A uniquely honest book about this brave woman. Coming from nowhere and fighting through life to find her wisdom, health and happiness. A must read for all those trying to gather their courage, having doubts. Sev will teach you how to believe in yourself and just go for it until you DO find your dreams and make them come true!

Kate Boyer
CEO & Co-Founder, Anatomie

Five stars for Never Give Up! Sev beautifully shares the gift of experience, love, and gratitude by touching our hearts and helping us appreciate our own essence and journey. A great contribution!

Dr. Manal Fakhoury
CEO, Vestech Partners

It is with honor that I recommend Sev's new book. As she describes her troublesome childhood and challenging journey to self-discovery and a better life, I am in constant awe of her dedication to her brother, Jacek, and of her wisdom and perseverance in achieving her dreams and ambitions. I feel lucky that I can now witness her growth and the wonderful person she has become; so loving, so inspirational, so fully present in her realization to cherish life's every moment. Her book is indeed a journey that we all can all learn from; dire struggles to inspiring successes, truly a feel-good read. Congratulations on a job well done my friend.

Jan Hargrave
Body Language Expert

Sev's journey towards healing her greatest pain and transforming it into grace, love, and hope has always been such an inspiration in my life! I truly believe that the most precious thing we can give each other is our truth. Every word in this book is filled with truth, love, and hope. This is not just a book to read; it's a path toward healing.

Thank you, Sev, for being willing to open your life, so that others can dive in and find the healing they need.

Just knowing you makes me want to become a better person, and now learning more about you through this book makes me believe I can!

So much love,

Dawn Watson
Forgiveness Coach Brasil

"All our dreams can come true,
if we have the courage to pursue them."

— *Walt Disney*

TABLE OF CONTENTS

FOREWORD

Opening your heart is expressing your purest beauty to this world. It's connecting to your inner strength and feeling it deep inside of you. Limits only exist in your imagination. I learned during all this journey that dreaming big or small makes all the difference in our life. Everything has its reason for being, even the storms in our lives are priceless gifts to explore our unique way of healing, coming back to love and expanding our unique destiny.

Believe in the magic of life's mystery. Above all, prepare for wonder. Explore it at every corner of your journey. You create it every day in your imagination, and you make it a reality through your daily, tiny actions - even the smallest. Each of us has a mission on this journey called life, and each experience is an integral part of this season . Live your life as if you only had one more day to live, bring more appreciation for what you have just right now, and it will take you on a whole new dimension ...

Dare to be courageous, be playful, embrace your shadows, savor life like a delicious homemade juice, and, most importantly, enjoy living in the now in each season of your colorful life , only that moment truly matters.

INTRODUCTION

My story is no better or worse than other people's. For a long time, I wanted to forget where I came from and who I was. I was ashamed of my past, of myself. I shed a lot of tears in silence, so that I wouldn't disturb anyone. Today, with a heart filled with gratitude, I feel an inner peace. I can now look back on my journey with kindness and a lot of admiration. I learned that not only could I be proud of my background, but also that it was the essential ingredient in my life's mission. Through my life story, I want to share with you how a painful and destructive experience can be turned into an extraordinary force that guides you towards infinite happiness. How faith, gratitude, and true forgiveness give us the courage to continue to believe and open the doors to the magic of the present moment. We are greater and stronger than we think.

My story only makes sense if I share it, and if I can help turn the course of events for even just one person on Earth, I would be the happiest woman. As Maya Angelou wrote, *"There is no greater agony than bearing an untold story inside you."*

I wrote with my heart, and I am so proud of this desire to share authentically what were my shadows for so many years . I ask for your indulgence for certain English sentences or a few mistakes I may make. My intention is to share with you a story of courage and resilience, which becomes a spark of hope for others to shine.

Welcome to my story,

*Thank you for taking your time to read this story and contributing by buying this book to help others believe in their worth and start building their dreams.

"Life is a gift, and it offers us the privilege, opportunity, and responsibility to give something back by becoming more."

– Tony Robbins

CHAPTER ONE

A Little Girl's Unshakable Faith

My Life in Poland

I was born on the 6th May, 1976 in Walbrzych, a small mining town in Southern Poland. It was the Communist era, a dark and difficult period. There was next to nothing in shops, and everything was rationed. Each month, Mum received a ration card and vouchers that enabled us to get a meager ration of sugar, flour, meat, and cigarettes. We survived, rather than lived.

Mum, my little brother, Jacek, and I lived in a very small house. We had no bathroom or toilet. We washed at the sink, and sometimes at night, in winter, we would use it to relieve ourselves. We had no boiler, so we had to heat water in a saucepan to wash or to cook. We had an old washing machine, called "Frania". It would wring out the clothes with a roller. I still remember the huge noise it made when it was on, and of course, it often broke down. Our other assets were rather scarce: a yellowish white piece of furniture whose doors didn't close properly, a table and four chairs made of recycled wood and a coal stove that we also ran in the spring to dry out the walls. Damp... It was an endless fight as it permeated everywhere, even our clothes and our hair. Water would seep in and peel off the paint; the walls were crumbling in places.

We all slept in the same bed. On the bedroom walls, there were moldy stains. As well as the damp, there was the cold. Winters in Poland were harsh. When it was minus twenty degrees outside, the temperature inside the house did not reach more than ten degrees. Then, we had to sleep with hot-water bottles and thick socks. The stove never quite managed to warm up the room. In winter, frost would form in the places where the glass had been damaged. During the great frosts, silhouettes would appear on the surface. I found that beautiful.

Mum, Jacek, and Me

My mother tried to fight this poverty all her life as best she could. She used to do housework and other odd jobs. She often changed jobs. Mum did what she could to take care of Jacek and me. Sometimes, she wasn't able to cook for us, because she was so drunk that she would fall asleep on the edge of the table, surrounded by glasses and empty bottles, the ashtray filled with cigarette butts. Very quickly, I learned to clean the table, throw away the bottles, air the room and put my mother to bed, fully clothed. In those moments, I was no longer a child - I was my mother's mother. And I would lie down beside her, my stomach empty, exhausted, and racked with disappointment.

At the age of three, I had to go to the orphanage, because Mum was ill: she had tuberculosis. There, I met my uncle Jan. Jan had come to the orphanage with his wife to adopt a child. I passed them in the hallway, and I asked them, "Whose parents are you?" Jan and his wife fell under my spell... and vice versa. They often came to see me. They wanted to adopt me. After some hesitation, Mum finally turned down the adoption. Uncle Jan did not leave my life, though, he has always looked out for me; he was my guardian angel...

When I was five, my brother, Jacek, was born. Such happiness, such a light in my life! His arrival was like a gift. Jacek changed my life forever.

Mum worked and was our sole carer most of the time. I looked after Jacek, and still went to school and took care of various household chores. Given my young age, I couldn't cope with Jacek's education, my schooling, and household chores. My mother found a boarding nursery where my eighteen-month-old brother would spend the week. On the weekend, we would take the bus to get him, and I often went to pick him up on my own. When we had to take him back to the crèche, after the weekend, I would be overcome with sadness. The house felt empty without him.

Jacek and I were often on our own. Mum would meet her friends after work, particularly after she got paid. I dreaded the beginning of the month, because she would spend her meager salary on alcohol. She drank more and more, and more and more often. Sometimes, she would start in the morning, and she would be drunk by lunchtime.

When she went out at night to meet her friends, I would beg her, with tears in my eyes, not to leave us alone. I was so scared. But she would go out anyway, promising she would be back soon. When Jacek and I were in bed, the noises from outside and the voices of passers-by were our lullaby. I would cuddle up against my little brother and pray to God. I would pray that nothing would happen to us, that no one would knock on the window. That Mum would come back soon.

I begged God, more than I prayed. I begged him to protect us, to give me the strength to work well in school and to have a better life. I did not dream of new dresses or dolls; I would just ask that Mum would stop drinking and smoking, and that she would spend more time with us. Jacek would be asleep beside me; I would watch out for every sound and would silently weep, so as not to wake him. I would fall asleep, exhausted with tiredness and grief. Mum often came home drunk, escorted, and would still be asleep the following morning. I already knew what to do for breakfast: heat the milk and make margarine toast when there was bread. Even though Mum was asleep, I was reassured that she was finally here, near us.

The Time I Suffered

I saw too many scenes of violence. My mother was with a man who abused her; he humiliated her and beat her. He would drag her across the floor like a mop. I was scared that one day, he might kill her. Her eyes were often swollen, her whole body was bruised, and she would stay on the floor for a long time. Each blow she received was a blow too far. I felt like I was receiving the same blows in my heart. I wanted to protect her. One day, I took her defense, and her friend pushed me violently. A little girl like me could do nothing against him.

Another day, my mother was with an uncle, another one in the series. Both had been drinking a lot of vodka. They had sex while my brother and I were in the same room. Fortunately, we were not in the same bed, and my brother was fast asleep. I was lying next to him. I heard everything; I put my hands over my ears, so I wouldn't hear their disgusting howls. I felt a deep sense of disgust. After he was finished with her, he came over to my bed. I felt his presence. I pretended to sleep. He started to touch me. He touched my body, my genitals. I wept bitterly. I pushed him away and I called my mother, crying. I hated her; I was angry against her because he carried on. He whispered in my ear with his breath that smelled of alcohol, "Don't worry; everything will be okay." I struggled harder, and it made him angry. He silenced me by putting his hand over my mouth. I bit him and I started to scream with all my strength, "Mummy, help me! " Hearing my voice, she woke up and she simply asked him to get out of our house. That was it. He went... she went back to bed; I was devastated. I felt completely broken from the inside. I wanted to disappear. I cried all night. This was the first time I felt truly alone, defenseless. I wanted to leave this place, to go away forever. I hated my mother so much. She never talked about what happened that night. Did she deliberately forget, or did she really not remember? I will never know. I have never told anyone. I decided to forget this story, out of shame.

In Survival Mode

Mum had a friend called Joseph; she really liked him, and this had been going on for some time. First, he lived with us, then, we moved in with him, because his house was bigger. He was twenty years her senior. They liked to drink together. Joseph was kind to me and Jacek. After some time, he started to raise his hand on Mum. He became very abusive to her when he was drinking. The neighbors did not say anything; they were used to it, and it never bothered anyone. Yet, one day, the violence nearly took my mother away.

I was eight, it was night time, around 10 p.m. Mum and Joseph were quarrelling, swear words were coming from both sides; they were screaming. He struck her again and again; Mum was helpless. Then he took the little metal coal shovel and hit my mother over the head and all over her body. It was a nightmare. I kept begging him to stop. I screamed, "You're going to kill her. You're going to kill my Mum! Stop it!" He stopped and pushed me, but he did not hit me. Mum was lying on the ground; blood was coming out of her nose. I panicked. Thank God, she was breathing and could still move a little. My mother was alive.

I ran into the bedroom. Jacek was asleep. I grabbed my schoolbag, opened the window, and went out in my pyjamas. It was snowing;

it was cold. I stopped the first passing car and I begged the people inside to go and help my Mum. The man and his passenger went into the house and hit Joseph. I did not follow them. I ran as fast as I could; I did not look ahead; I was scared to go home, scared of the idea that I had called strangers for help. Almost a mile further, I stopped and got on a bus. I was lucky that there was a night bus available. I went to my aunt Krystyna's.

This exceptional woman was always there for me. She, too, was like a guardian angel in my life. Since I was little, she always helped us. Despite the fact that there is no blood relation between us, she was a friend of our late grandmother's, she was my aunt in my heart. When I arrived at Krystyna's, I threw myself into her arms and told her everything. I cried and cried. With her soft voice, she reassured and comforted me. I found comfort and tenderness with her. It was so good to let go in someone's arms. Krystyna prepared a bed for me, and I fell asleep, exhausted. The next day, I was terrified at the thought of returning home. Krystyna went to see my mother to tell her I was with her, safe. I ended up staying there for three days. My aunt took care of me. When I returned home, I saw how Mum's face was damaged. She suffered enormously from his assault. She was not happy that I had left the house, but she did not scold me. Seeing her in such a state made me weep. I felt ashamed for having abandoned her and my brother.

We went back to our little house. It was not perfect, we lived very modestly, but we felt safer. Despite the beatings and the violence, Mum did not leave Joseph. They got back together shortly after.

This episode of my life has had a huge impact on me, due to its unprecedented violence, but it was also one of the most beautiful gifts that life has given me: this unshakable faith that has been growing ever since.

A New Life at the Orphanage

At only nine years old, I chose my own life. Deep inside, I so wanted to have a better life, a life like other children's lives. I never stopped believing; this hope was in my daily prayers.

Mum had deserted the house for the umpteenth time. She had been gone for three days without a sign. This time, I had no more food to give to Jacek. I still remember the last piece of bread that we ate the night before: bread toasted on the stove with sugar. I had a little hiding place, I would keep a few coins just in case, but it was empty, and we had to eat something. My stomach was hurting, and I was disappointed I was not able to feed my brother that morning. I took my brother to kindergarten, and then, I went to my school. As usual, I didn't show anything, and besides, no one was aware of anything. I was good at hiding our problems; I didn't want anyone to say bad things about my mother. But this time, I cracked. Hunger was stronger than shame. I asked my teacher if she had something to eat, I felt weak. I was crying non-stop; I was terribly ashamed to tell her our life—I felt guilty for exposing Mum. The school immediately warned the social worker who had been following me since my first stay at the orphanage. Police and special services for children then came to take us straight to the children's home (the place where children await the court's judgment deciding whether they are going to the orphanage or going back home).

A few days later, Mum came to visit us. I felt terribly guilty; it hurt me to see her cry. My heart swung between guilt and sadness. The nights were short. I didn't sleep well, I had nightmares, and I had chronic tachycardia attacks. My body was sending me messages: my little heart had lived through so many emotions for so many years. After a few weeks, a feeling of serenity appeared. Then, the shame and anger eased. I found peace.

The children's home was heaven for us. It was quiet, no arguments, no alcohol, and no violence. We had real meals at fixed times; I didn't have to worry about finding a way to eat. Watching my little brother run and play with other children in the park gave me so much joy.

Nine months later, the tribunal made their decision: we were sent to the orphanage. Mum was sad; I imagine that she blamed me. I felt guilty to cause her grief. I was full of remorse, but I had made a choice; the choice of a better life, because, inside me, I knew that Jacek and I deserved to have a life like all children. I never stopped believing it. It was the first time that I felt in my heart that I had made the right decision.

Life in the orphanage was not always easy. There were a lot of rules, and we had to be disciplined, which we had not been used to at home! We had to adapt and learn to live in a community. We had to get up early. We had to make our beds very specifically. But I was so happy that for the first time in my life, I had my own bed. It was delicious to feel the smell of crisp, clean sheets. We began the day with community work: vacuuming, polishing the floor, taking the laundry baskets to the laundry. Then, we could get washed, in a real bathroom at that! We had a shower—which was often cold—but it was such a pleasure to feel the water flowing over my body and feel cool in the morning! I enjoyed this new life. I learned rigor. At last, I had a quiet home, a place where I could do my homework and where I could see my brother having enough to eat and time to play with other kids.

Each situation in life offers you choices. Sometimes, you hesitate because you are afraid. Deep inside, there is this little voice that guides you. This intuition, this force more powerful than you, guiding your steps. Deciding to go to the orphanage was a difficult choice. From the moment I made this decision, I was already creating my new destiny. Determination and faith stayed with me during all the way.

With each decision, something new again awaits you. New doors open. All you need to do is to listen to the voice of your heart, where this divine force resides. The challenges you meet along the way have been chosen for you to help you grow, to help your face your fear and own your truth; they are part of your unique journey. They are part of your life's destiny. These are your gifts, even if you don't know it yet. You need to embrace them, honor the teaching of each of them, and welcome your new you.

"The world has enough beautiful mountains and meadows, spectacular skies, and serene lakes. It has enough lush forests, flowered fields, and sandy beaches. It has plenty of stars and the promise of a new sunrise and sunset every day. What the world needs more of is people to appreciate and enjoy it."

– Michael Josephson

CHAPTER TWO

The Magic of Appreciating Life's Little Gifts

Life is a blessing; it gives you wonderful gifts each day. You only need to know how to catch them and appreciate them. In fact, everything is a matter of perception. People often say to me: "You're too *peace and love*, come down to Earth!", "Life is complicated, and you're smiling, as if there was nothing amiss!", or "What makes you so happy? Something special must have happened for you laugh like that?"

Do you really need to have specific reasons to enjoy life? To be happy? I don't think so. In fact, these questions make me smile, and I welcome them with compassion. When you communicate your *joie de vivre*, it has a tremendous impact on the people around you. Open your heart; life whispers messages of happiness each and every day. When you are in perfect communion with life, you will feel this human warmth, these gifts of nature. No matter what the weather is outside, no matter the chaos in your life, you will always find something beautiful to appreciate just for a moment.

I marvel at the present moment and the small gifts that life offers me each and every day, because they may not happen tomorrow. Every second, every minute is a renewal of breath and feelings. There is no time to waste: what must happen will happen, we have no control on the outside world.

Focus your energy on admiring what is simply beautiful around you. The present moment is only one that you really own, because you are just one of them. Learning from life every day's challenges reveal their real meaning, and I am no longer afraid to be afraid; it's part of growth, but I can still have some moment of tiny appreciation, which really helps me to move forward challenges. I know that deep down, I am resourceful, and that happiness is never far away.

This way of seeing things is a majestic gift I inherited from my early childhood and which has strengthened over time.

Tasty Memories

Garlic, a Culinary Memory Like No Other!

I remember as if it was yesterday how happy I was to look after my little brother, Jacek. When Mum would leave us on our own to go to work, or to go out drinking with her friends, I would make us toast on the stove that I would then rub with garlic. Yummy! It smelled so good throughout the house... I would eat the remaining ends of the garlic. I loved how it stung my mouth. I would make delicious tea with lemon. Jacek enjoyed it and would say, "I want more; it's good!". Seeing him eat made me feel so good. I was just happy to see him enjoy his food, and I was proud of myself: my little brother was no longer hungry.

The Taste of a Spring Strawberry

I still remember the delicious taste of strawberries freshly bought by Mum on payday. They were so juicy, so sweet. Mum would then prepare our favorite meal: toast with butter and strawberries sprinkled with sugar. I will never forget this moment of pure delight. We were so happy. Jacek and I would savor each bite slowly, soaking in this perfect mixture of spring, this gift of nature. Writing these words, my mouth waters!

Delicious Mashed Potatoes

At the age of about six, I learned to peel potatoes. I would often graze my fingers, and there would only be half of the potato left, but it was such a pleasure to have done it myself! Watching my little brother enjoying homemade mashed potatoes, a hot meal, when Mum wasn't there, was a real treat, my reward.

Juicy Oranges

We were so happy when Christmas came. I particularly remember one day when it was snowing. Everything was white. Jacek and I were terribly excited. Mum had gone to do some shopping, and we wanted to surprise her by decorating the Christmas tree. We made a beautiful garland with scraps of colored paper and tin foil. We also hung some sweets in the tree. Of course, we could not help but to taste some in secret. When Mum finally came back, there was a surprise; she had bought a kilo of beautiful juicy oranges. It was so rare to have them in those days. We could only have them for Christmas, and they were very expensive. Mum was hardly through the door when we jumped on the bag containing oranges, so we could taste a juicy piece. Their delicious aroma filled the whole house! It was a moment of pure happiness. I still have the taste of that sweet flesh in my mouth. It was such a pleasure to keep the dried orange peel a long time after Christmas. This extended the magic of Christmas in our little house.

The Magic of Christmas

On Christmas Eve, someone knocked on the door. We were not expecting any visitors. With Mum's approval, I opened the door. Before me, there were two young men holding two packages filled with candy, chocolate, oranges, apples, cakes and small toys. My eyes sparkled, my brother ran to me, and, of course, he raised his arms to get his gift. Mum asked who had sent us this. One of the young men replied, smiling, "This is from Santa Claus. He left us this package for you. Merry Christmas!" Then, they gave us the two packages and left. I was so happy. Jacek was already eating a chocolate, and my mother smiled, her eyes filled with tears. Her smile was so genuine, so pure. I thought to myself, *Oh, thank you, God. Santa, thank you for not forgetting us.* After that, I no longer had any doubt that Santa Claus did exist!

Since that day, Christmas has been to me a symbol of divine gift, of sharing, of compassion. Nothing is more beautiful than to allow the poorest families to enjoy the magic of Christmas like everyone else. Every year, especially at this time, it is an honor and a real pleasure for me to help others. I buy food that I offer to the poorest. I also share my time and gifts; I send money to someone who really needs it. Last Christmas, I had coal delivered to my aunt in Poland, so that she could heat her house all winter. The most magical thing was that the driver was kind enough to deliver coal on Christmas Eve, the 24th of December. I was so happy to hear her voice on the phone, she cried with joy. The deliveryman, too, contributed to make this wonderful woman happy. Creating even just a spark of joy in someone's life makes me so happy.

Rationing, a Unique Event

During the Communist era, everything was rationed in stores. There was almost nothing on the shelves. Although some had a little money, they had no choice, because the stores were empty. People would barter. We had to settle for the month's ration card, even if we ran out of supplies, even if we had the means to buy an additional card. I still remember what it was like at the butcher's when the meat arrived. At five o'clock in the morning, everyone would rush to queue in order to try to get a small piece of meat, or just a bit of sausage. It was a nice change from the lard we spread on a slice of bread. We still enjoyed this lard on fresh bread. It was delicious! We had to queue very early in the morning to make sure we could buy a piece of meat; most of the time, there was nothing on the shelves, barely two hours after opening. It was an event, because neighbors would meet in the queue. It was a pleasure to see the shelves full, just for a moment. The abundance, the fresh sausage smell delighted me. The children loved these moments: we would keep a space for our mothers; it was fun, in a way. It was a time when we were all together and happy to be together.

The Scents of My Childhood

The Purity of the Poppy

In summer, I loved walking through the plains not far from the house. There was a multitude of wildflowers all over the fields. Mum taught me to make flower wreaths. I would pick little daisies, and I would plait pretty crowns for Mum and me. I found it amazing to admire up close the extraordinary beauty of the poppies. Since I was a child, I have always admired this flower. It is the perfect combination of blood-red leaves and the black tips of the finely drawn, small seeds. I remember that Sunday morning when I was watching them. It was very warm. I can still feel the breath of the warm breeze on my skin. As a child, these gifts of nature made me so happy. Without knowing it, I was already in a form of meditation and communion with life.

The Taste of the First Kiss

Ah, my first kiss... what joy and excitement! The funny thing is how I learned to kiss. I was with my girlfriend, Mariola, talking about the boys we liked. We spoke timidly. Neither of us dared to say that we didn't know how to kiss, but at the same time, we were dying to know. At one point, I plucked up the courage to finally ask her, "Do you know how to kiss with the tongue?" Looking slightly disturbed, she said, "I don't really know, but I've seen my parents turn their tongue in each other's mouth, and that's it." I replied, "How are you supposed to learn that? If a boy ever wants to kiss one of us, we won't know how to do it, and he'll laugh at us!"

So, we tried! We had such a laugh! At first, we were embarrassed, but after a few instructions, we did it. Mariola and I kissed with the tongue. We decided that this would be our secret. It was funny, and it still makes me laugh today.

My First Pair of Pink Shoes

Each month, my uncle Jan would visit me. He never entered the house. I think he didn't want Mum to feel intimidated by him. He did not make her uncomfortable by entering a messy house that reeked of cigarette smoke. He always had someone else call me. I would meet him in his car parked down the yard, and we would chat for a while. He was happy to see me, and he always asked about the family. Sometimes, I saw tears in his eyes. I didn't understand why at the time.

I remember one day in particular. It was my birthday; I had just turned seven. Jan took banknotes out of his pocket and said, "Severyna, there, this is for you. I know you need new shoes. Please, take this money and go and choose a pair of shoes that you like with your Mum." I looked at him and thanked him. I looked at my feet and my pair of blue trainers. The sole was peeling off, and the big toe was beginning to pop out. I felt a little embarrassed to take his money, but I needed it so much. I thanked him again from the bottom of my heart, and my eyes filled with tears.

When I returned home, I told Mum everything, and I gave her the money, saying, "Mum, my uncle gave me this money to buy shoes, but I know that you need it to buy food. Take it, it's for you." It made me even happier to give her this money, to be able to help buy food for the family. A kind of inner pride came over me. She had tears in her eyes. She took me in her arms, saying, "Thank you, darling, thank you. You can't imagine how much your help is valuable. It's your money, my little girl, and you're giving it to me, I don't know what to say." We both ended up crying with joy.

Once again, my uncle had come at the right time. We did some shopping and then, Mum said, "Let's go, darling. Let's choose a nice pair of shoes for you; there will be enough money to make you happy. After all, it's your birthday."

So, we took the bus. I was so excited. At the store, I fell in love with a pair of pink moccasins. It looked to me like they had been waiting for me. I touched them. They smelled of new leather. I finally tried them on. I felt beautiful and light, like a little butterfly. The next day at school, I was so proud to show off my first pair of new shoes. This pair of shoes was a magical moment of my childhood, a symbol filled with deep meaning. So many things are more important than material things.

Tender Memories with Mum

I remember all my precious moments with Mum. When she was sober, she was so beautiful and understanding. To make me laugh out loud, she would make faces, she would frown, bend her lips, and I would burst out laughing. At night, when Jacek was asleep between us, we would each read our books. I loved reading Andersen's fairy tales; these stories made me dream. When I didn't understand a word, I loved asking her for the meaning. I think she was proud to see me devour books. As if by magic, Mum would sometimes bring out our favorite sweets with salted butter caramel, and I would enjoy this delicious moment with her. I could see her eyes shine with happiness. She felt fulfilled to spend these moments with her children.

I will always remember the way she would pat my small head laid on her lap. I could feel her warmth. I felt like I belonged there; I felt loved and protected. I will always keep these rare moments inside of me, and I enjoy them for what they are: magic moments, true treasures. I am so happy to be able to keep these images in my heart forever; they are so precious.

I thank my mother every day for the opportunity to have lived this life and no other. It allowed me to become independent very early on, to know how to get by, no matter what happens. It also allowed me to appreciate life's every little gift. I realized that living a great human adventure is primarily taking care of others. Somehow, it is because of this suffering that I feel compassion and better understand other women's suffering today. Fear and loneliness felt in extreme moments are sometimes difficult to share.

I've come to realize that it is in moments of deep pain that the inner strength awakens within us. I am certain of one thing: the deep desire and the daily small steps of courage transform our lives and awaken this dormant force. This lesson, I owe to you, Mummy, thank you.

The Flow of Dance

Dancing is a pure expression of my soul. This connection between my body and my inner feelings helps me to release any tension, any fear, any stories. I feel alive and just in flow with the moment. When I dance, I don't think about anything; I let go of my body, and my soul finds its way to express my love for life in that moment . My body knows where to go; I don't need to control, just follow my instinct . I marvel at the natural movement of my hips, my arms. I feel alive when I move, just as easy as when I breathe. When I dance, I feel light, bubbly. I feel my energy turn into a deep vibration. After that, anything can happen. I'm ready; dance is my escape. Sometimes, when I feel sad or when anger overcomes me, I turn up the volume, and I disconnect from everything. I express my emotions through movement, and—as if by magic—I naturally reconnect to my inner peace. When I dance, I explore this feeling of lightness in my heart. I feel an irresistible connection to this flow of energy through my entire body, which gives me a feeling of well-being. I feel joyful. Sometimes, a small tear runs down my cheek, and I shudder. Often, when I'm in the car listening to music, I dance at the wheel. I move, and I sing. Some people wave at me and laugh.

Dance is my secret weapon, it helps me express all colors of my emotions. Each movement gives me this capacity to expand my presence here and now ; my whole being is connected to life through dance. It's like freedom and endless aliveness in this moment.

CHAPTER THREE

The Liberating Power of Forgiveness

"Love heals. Heals and liberates. I use the word love, not meaning sentimentality, but a condition so strong that it may be that which holds the stars in their heavenly positions and that which causes the blood to flow orderly in our veins."

Maya Angelou

The most priceless gift that can be given to your loved ones is simply to forgive them. Forgiveness will never change your story of the past, only your perception will . I know it's not always easy. Sometimes, it feels more painful than the wound we suffered to forgive the one who inflicted it. Feeling pain holds us back and, above all, makes us feel disconnected from the present. We constantly spend our time in that specific souvenir and create all those thoughts, and so, we make that suffering alive within . Finding our deepest peace comes only through a deep and sincere pardon.

Treat yourself to the gift of letting go and listen to your heart for this profound truth. It has so much to tell you and teach you about your own life and the meaning you give to each story. Life offers you the most beautiful gift, your heart, and it works hard every day: it beats to keep you alive and passes on all sorts of emotions. In the middle of all these human emotions what you truly need is experiencing the feeling of each of them and coming back to the truth of your presence: your love and your compassion for yourself. We all have the choice to stay in pain with the constant weight of the past or to free ourselves to be free to love, move on, and live in the present moment, the only one we truly own .

Forgiving Mum

It was October 2009. My half-sister told me that Mum was not well at all. She was staying in bed; she couldn't even get up to go to the bathroom; she was bleeding. It was undignified to leave a woman lying in her own urine, in a damp house, without care. No one dared do anything, so I acted as fast I could. I asked to call the ambulance immediately to take her to the hospital. Mum arrived at the hospital in a critical condition; her liver was in bad way, her body was swollen, and she was extremely thin. At the hospital, the doctors said that she didn't have long.

I felt the need to call her. I didn't want to wait to be in Poland to talk to her. I asked my brother to join me at the office. On the phone, Mum's voice was very faint, but she was smiling. She was happy to hear us. Without saying a word, I felt warmth in my heart; the eight-thousand-kilometer distance between us was just a perception, because I did not feel any distance at that point. I was so moved, I felt so much compassion, my stomach tightened. I was in so much pain for her. Mum had given me life, and today, she was alone in that hospital, far away from me physically and yet closer than ever before.

I cried with tears of joy. I felt an immense relief; I felt warmth, a kind of energy that was released and emanated from her through the phone. She was crying and smiling at the same time. I told her about her grandchildren, Kelyan and Lea. I had sent her pictures of them through a family member's email. I wanted her to imprint the image of her granddaughter in particular, whom she had not had time to meet. Mum was so happy. I told her how much I loved her. I saw my childhood flash before my eyes. Mum, weakened, whispered a few words and was trying to apologize. At times, she could barely speak. I felt her powerful love during that moment, her vulnerability made her so beautiful. I imagined her through the phone, so authentic, with all the strength of a mother and powerlessness in the face of the disease; it made that moment unique.

I gradually felt pressure being released from my stomach. In an instant, I was breathing more deeply. I was more serene, despite the situation. I felt a great love for this woman who had given me life. Just at that moment, her little voice whispered, "I love you, my daughter. Forgive me for all the harm I've caused you. I've always loved you." That moment was so intense that my whole body was crying with joy. My brother and I were so at one in tears and deep compassion for Mum. I didn't even realize, at the time, the gift that was given to me. In hindsight, enjoying this feeling of deep forgiveness with my mother was simply extraordinary. I guess she, too, felt a great deliverance. This event made me feel what true unconditional love means and how quickly we can change this inner feeling when we share compassion, just a presence of love.

A few days later, I was off to Poland. Mum's health was getting worse. On the plane that was taking me to her, I became ill with bronchitis. I had a stopover in Paris for the night of the 3rd to 4th of November, as there were no connections for Poland on the same day. That night, I woke up suddenly, feverish. I couldn't stop coughing, and I had trouble breathing. That night, the ER doctor told me I had a serious lung inflammation. The next morning, Jacek called me and gave me the sad news: "Sev, Mum died last night." Straightaway, I asked him what time she had gone. He answered, "Between three and four in the morning." I was completely astonished: Mum had come to say goodbye, I'm sure. I realized at that moment that everything is a question of energy.

We are all connected by a powerful force whose existence we underestimate. The more we share this unconditional love and compassion for those who have hurt us, the more we free our hearts and we have the capacity to feel the energies of the people who love us, no matter where they are.

Once I had forgiven her, Mum was able to connect to my soul and she came to visit me before her transition. There were no more barriers. I felt free, because she went free. I felt her soul, just the truth of her gift, her courageous being who just gave her best.

Forgiving My Husband

I've been married since the 6th October 2006. I had a lovely wedding, and we founded a real family, as I had never had in my childhood. For once in my life, I felt I could settle down. I was happy and I completely trusted my husband. I felt good; I felt safe. Anthony is a wonderful man. He is so caring and a great dad.

Just after Christmas 2009, I found out that my husband had been cheating on me for months, or even a year. I felt completely lost, devastated, and ashamed. I felt betrayed by the man in whom I had absolute trust. We had lived through so much and so many challenges. I received a deep blow to the heart whilst I was already trying to cope with Mum's recent death. I suffered enormously. I asked him to leave the house; I couldn't bear to see him—it reminded me of his lies. I hated him. It took several weeks before I managed to calm myself.

The decision was in my hands. Once again, I had to make the decision myself. I was scared, and I felt so fragile. I needed time to think. I didn't know where to start.

I had a taste of what many women go through. I'm not the only one to have experienced this, and I certainly won't be the last! In those moments, you feel fear and humiliation. You lose sense of everything and you just want to disappear. You feel deeply wounded.

Then, one day, I woke up, and I'd had enough of watching myself suffer like this. I'd had enough of wasting away and being a victim of my own choices or indecisiveness. I could not remain in this vegetative state; it was unbearable. I had to do something. At that time, Tony Robbins's book resurfaced. I had already read it, and I don't know why, but I dove back into it at this difficult time of my life. Should we separate? What would then become of our children and this family, so precious in my eyes? I sat with a cup of citrus green tea, and I put music on. For hours, I wrote what I really wanted to experience in my life and what I would never accept again, what I liked about this man and what I did not like. After a few months of reflection and many tears, I decided to forgive him. Something inside of me told me this story had to continue and our relationship should be given a second chance.

I realized that I loved him, but deep down, I still had doubts and a lot of grief. I needed time to trust him again, something had been broken.

I realized during this process my own mistakes. It was not about him, but the way I was expecting things from him and never clearly had courage to tell him what I really wanted to feel being with him . What I really wanted like a woman . I provided to him everything I thought it was good for him instead of giving him what he really needed .

We both agreed to meet this challenge together. It was worth giving our relationship another chance. We learned how to communicate again, to express our needs to one another.

The day I forgave my husband, I did not yet know I had just given myself the greatest gift of my life. Now I know that everything happens for a reason. Without knowing it, I received another priceless gift in my life as a woman. I learned over time to listen to a man's needs, to understand his language of love. I discovered how important is to come from that place of wholeness myself, nobody can really fulfill my needs if I don't nourish them first. Nobody was responsible of the way I felt : I was , and the first step was to have courage to tell him the truth of my feeling .Love is not something we expect from someone else; it's place where you give first and you share one hundred percent, without expecting anything in return, without judging. To love is to move forward together through the storms.It's not always easy , but it's part of life growth . To love unconditionally is to love even when it hurts, to know how to forgive with compassion. Because we all do our best with our level of consciousness , and when we really love it's always time to learn and embrace the differences, and to appreciate what is already beautiful in other person. The most priceless lesson I learned is that nobody belongs to anybody , we are just here to learn from each others and to become a better version of ourself. It's never about the other person; it's always a reflection of our own inner conflict , inner resistance , our own perception of the world.

Often, the most painful experiences give us access to a higher level of awakening; they enable us to understand ourselves, even though it's very hard at the time. But nothing lasts forever, including pain. Without knowing it, I turned this painful experience into a force, a beautiful story that, ultimately, had a huge impact on my life, but also on my family, my husband, and my loved ones. During the following months, I decided to take care of myself and invest into my personal development. This is how I attended my first seminar, *Unleash the Power Within*, with Anthony Robbins, in Rimini in 2011. For twelve years, I had dreamed of attending one of his seminars and seeing him in person. This event changed my life forever .

Forgiving My Father

What I am most proud of is to have spent one of most beautiful birthdays with my father in the hospital. He was in his final phase of stomach cancer and had metastases everywhere. He was in palliative care at the hospital in Valenciennes, in northern France. I was in Guadeloupe with my family when I received a phone call from my stepmother, informing me that Dad could be going very soon, that the cancer had spread, and the chemo no longer had any effect. I got onto the first plane.

For the whole flight, I was anxious. I didn't know how to describe this feeling; my stomach was tense, and I also felt nostalgic. I remembered a few moments with my dad, in particular the day when he had come to get me in Poland from the orphanage, when I was fourteen years old. He didn't have to, after all. He had not had any news from me, nor my mother, since my birth, but he had decided to assume his role as a father. I also remembered when he arrived at my wedding.

This was after a ten-year absence. He had kicked me out of his house when I was eighteen, and I didn't see him again until I was twenty-eight. Despite everything, I had invited him to my wedding, having always dreamed that he would walk me down the aisle. And he did come. All these memories were coming back to me one by one. For some strange reason, I cried during the flight, aware that I did not really know him. We had lived alongside each other during those years, without really developing real ties. But something more powerful reminded me something crucial: this man gave me life.

Without him, I would not be here, and when I lingered on that thought, joy returned to my heart instantly. I stopped asking myself stupid questions, trying to change the world.

When I arrived at the hospital, after a ten-hour flight, my father greeted me with a smile that I will never forget. My stepmother told me she had not seen him smile like that for a long time. I spent four days beside him. He was in a lot of pain, but he said nothing, as usual. Dad was not a talkative man.

On the 6th of May, 2014, I received my greatest birthday gift, another wonderful gift from God. As I was watching him that day, I saw the joy in his eyes. I took his hands, which were cold and numb. We looked into each other's eyes, without saying a word, for several minutes. Our eyes were smiling; we were connected through our hearts. Tears of joy were streaming down our cheeks. We were enjoying the eternity of that instant. I saw my father under a different light, and it was beautiful: the beauty of a father. I took him in my arms, and he said into my ear, "I love you, my daughter." He had never yet said it to me. I was so happy, I cried, I was being released from all the sorrows related to my past with my father. And he was also gently releasing his heart.

That day, nobody came to visit him, and I am forever grateful to my stepmother for allowing us to be just me and my dad . I felt a moment of pure joy when Dad told me how proud he was of me for all that I had achieved without his assistance or his support. With tears in his eyes, He admitted that he regretted all the harm that he had caused me. My father, who never said anything, would not cease speaking. I'm sure, deep down, that he never recovered from kicking me out of the house at the age of eighteen.

I told him that I had been very hurt at the time, but that because of it, I had become who I am. I learned to get by in life, and I sincerely thanked him for everything. I had forgiven him long ago, but, that day, that forgiveness carried a deeper meaning. I felt his love in his purest expression of looking at me with this little spark of compassion.

While Dad was asleep, I went downstairs and looked for something to eat in a small shop, and I saw a little toy bee. It immediately caught my eye: "That's for Dad." When he woke up, I offered him this little Maya-the-Bee. He was so happy, he laughed. He took the bee and began to make it fly, to hug it like a child who gets carried away by the magic of the moment. We actually both laughed like children. Then, I told him that I would always be at his side, like this little bee, twirling, in awe of life. A tear ran down his cheek, and he thanked me from the heart with a look full of fatherly love. He closed his eyes again, as he was under morphine. I took his cold hands, and, with a little almond oil, I massaged them. He let me do it with a tranquil smile and fell asleep like a little boy, finally at peace. I enjoyed that moment. Everything in the room seemed large, delicious, luminous; I felt like a divine presence among us. I felt the force of forgiveness in every cell of my body. Dad had freed his heart, and he was the happiest man that day. As for me, I was the luckiest little girl; I was overcome with love and compassion. This connection changed the way I saw my father forever. I freed my heart from the weight of the past. And so did he.

Thank you, God, for allowing me to live this father-daughter reunion and finally hear the man who never expressed his feelings. He told me he still loved my mother. His regrets remain forever engraved in my heart. Thank you, Dad, for opening up to me, thank you for this gift. Thanks to you, I learned to never have regrets. I want to bite into life, learn, try new experiences, follow my deepest dreams. I'm not afraid of making mistakes, I am going to create my own life with a meaning I decide to, not suffer , just take a little, tiny action .

This is what I learned from this experience: our perceptions and the resulting emotions have a direct link with the ultimate forgiveness that we are able—or unable—to give to others. Whenever I have forgiven, I have freed myself a little more, like a little bird out of its cage: my cage opened, and the bird flew away and was able to start flying higher and higher.

Forgiving Myself

I thought I had forgiven myself several years ago, but there was always something that weighed on my heart, unconsciously. I made other people responsible for my happiness, I always felt this fear paralyzed myself when I was living through an uncomfortable situation. I inflicted such resistance throughout my body, so many tears shed for so many years in silence, so much pain inside of my heart. I was afraid of not being up to it, to disappoint someone. Step by step, I finally realized that I was punishing myself, and it was time to reconnect to my true self and truly forgive myself. But I didn't know how. I had enough of feeling various pains in my stomach, in my heart, in my whole body: constipation, stomach ulcers, bulimia, asthenia, palpitations, nightmares, phobia of knives, suicide attempt. My body was talking to me, but I didn't hear; I had to learn how to listen to it. All these pains were related to stories which I unconsciously had decided to hide deep inside of me to protect myself.

In order to grow, I had to let it go from my past stories ,but I didn't know how to start , what to do to heal this inner child to feel free of this pain.

Then after all this years of holding on, suffering inside, crying in silence, I finally understood that I had forgotten to forgive myself. This true release, this ultimate forgiveness, was like a rebirth of my soul. For the first time, I felt this kind of compassion to myself and this grace in everything around me; I finally feel myself just enough and so courageous enough, I feel alive again.

Through this liberating power of being compassionate with myself, I feel that I fully exist, aligned with my true nature of just being me; it's like by looking through eyes of love, I see the world around me from a different perspective. Forgiveness has completely changed the way of connecting myself with life. Today, free of this constant judgement towards myself, released from this weight from my oldest memories, I feel like a ray of sunshine shining back after a big storm. Deciding to give a different meaning to my old story, it was like a rebirth and a new journey began.

So, don't wait until it's too late; each day, each little step matters. Don't allow all regrets and this inner dialogue destroy your unique expression of your soul. You have so much to offer from that space of love . You will feel rising this peaceful feeling of belonging, this inner calmness, free of all judgement, living just in present moment. A heavy heart self-destructs. Forgive yourself—it is the best gift you can give yourself to live fully in the now. To forgive is to free yourself from this inner permanent fight; it is to connect with the present moment without judgment . Without true forgiveness, you cannot move forward; you will always miss a piece of this beauty of life by this disconnection of the source of love. Everything we do in this life experience has a deepest meaning. Every action, every thought, every attitude has an impact on someone around us. This is one of the most powerful keys to success in our lives. Forgiveness is just a matter of choice, to live in love with oneself. Look at the impact of that choice on the lives of your children, your family, your friends, everyone around you. Just think how, in turn, you could impact the lives of your loved ones just because forgiveness has freed you from an emotional weight that was stopping you from thriving .

The beauty of forgiveness is accessible at any moment in our journey. Only we have this capacity to decide and step to that unknown experience of freeing ourselves from the past memories, and giving space to this rising feeling of peace in the now. Taking this decision takes courage, because we have to change all our behaviors. We have to become aware that suffering is not who we are; it's just our obsessive thinking of ourselves; it's a survival instinct. It's a constant separation of our true potential, of our true being.

It's not easy for sure, but it's the only way, the only way to start the journey of letting go of suffering and giving another meaning to our life story .Only from that space of acceptance and self-compassion can we transform our quality of life and take our lives to the next level. We can change the course of our life just by taking that ultimate decision. We can only grow and magnify our authentic self from this ultimate inner peace.

"Forgiveness is not always easy. At times, it feels more painful than the wound we suffered, to forgive the one that inflicted it. And yet, there is no peace without forgiveness."

- Marianne Williamson

CHAPTER FOUR

The Magic of Life Works Through Courage and Determination

" I learned that courage was not the absence of fear, but the triumph over it. The brave man is not he who does not feel afraid, but he who conquers that fear."

- Nelson Mandela

What is courage? For me, it's not giving up, even at the most difficult times. The bigger the challenges, the more you develop your resilience and this extraordinary ability to give the best of yourself, to tap into your inner resources. And by giving the best you can, you receive so much more from life . By adapting to circumstances, you can navigate through life's strong currents. But courage is also accepting your lack of experience in specific situations . You must let go of what you cannot control. Then, with patience and faith the solution might just show the end of its nose! You are guided when you let courage be your companion , because you connect to the present. Your desire to achieve something, to succeed can then be fulfilled. It can sometimes take time. We have all inside us this extraordinary capacity to achieve the impossible. It is enough to have the courage to accept that, sometimes, we can suffer because of it, too. But there is something we can do: listen to our heart and let it be our guide.

Going Through Life with Courage and Determination

I've often given up; I've often told myself that I wouldn't be able to do this or that, or I wasn't enough for doing this or that. I would compare myself to others, thinking that they were better than me, that they had more money, more success than me. I forgot what I had achieved in my life, and I always told myself that my experience was nothing special compared to others who suffered terribly. I was also ashamed to share my life: ashamed of what the others were going to think of me and of my family. I was afraid of being judged, afraid of being rejected and being left alone. I so easily forgot the courage I had shown going through some of many challenges…

Thank you, God. You give me this courage to show up to my unique life and to allow myself to see the beauty of my soul in the middle of the darkest moment. Step by step, I have learned how to look at my life with more compassion. I stopped punishing myself, and continually doubting my own capacity to shine. I understood that feeling completely depressed or happy depended on only one person: me. Me and the story I decided to tell to myself.

So be yourself. Accept yourself with your qualities and your weaknesses; you are here to learn and to experience by being you just the way you are . Have the courage to show who you really are. Perfection does not exist; it is an illusion. Every day, you learn from your mistakes; they are experiences that enable you to become better versions of yourself. Take the time to simply say, "Okay, everything is going to be fine." There will be always a solution, even in the darkest situations. I've lived through difficult times, but this courage to take a decision and move forward has given me this strength and the support I needed to keep going and stay focused on what is the most important to my heart.

Try just for one moment to connect with what scares you the most. All these emotions of fear, shame, disappointment, and anger are part of your essence, my gorgeous; don't avoid facing them. They give you strength. Don't reject them anymore; they are your internal clock. Listen to them—they have so much to tell you.

They constantly guide you to your truth .The more you reject them, the more you resist, so you disconnect yourself from what is most mysterious in you, your truth , your radiant flow of your soul .

Your vulnerability is your wisdom; it's your deepest power.

Dare to be you. You have so much to give from this place of authenticity.

Departure for a New Life: a New Country and a Father, At Last.

On the 16th of June, 1990, a new adventure started. I had waited for this moment for such a long time. The adventure had actually begun three years earlier, when at the age of 11, I decided to write to my father. This desire had been eating at me for a long time already. I wanted to know this man, to discover his face, who he was. As I listened to a piece by Enya, "Sail Away", in my room at the orphanage, I let my heart speak. I wrote without stopping. I was moved, I felt transported by this energy. I so wanted to know my daddy, to put a face to his name. When I was small, I had often been told that I looked like him. I wrote, pushed by the hope that he would answer, that I could meet him one day. Three months later, I received the long-awaited letter. I could not believe my eyes. I was so happy that I showed his letter to everybody. It was a happy day: my father really did exist.

That day, I was nervous. My father was coming to take me to live with him in France. The big day had finally come—I was waiting for him impatiently. I could not stop looking out of the window. I was curious to discover my father's face for the first time. Each minute seemed like an eternity. A car with a foreign number plate had just pulled into the yard; it was a distraction for us children, to see a foreign car in our area, and even more so at the orphanage. Children from various groups ran towards me to tell me, "Sev, your father is here!" And dad arrived! My hands were moist; I joined him in the corridor. His beard was real, like on the few photographs I had of him. I could not manage to believe that he had come to take me to live with him and his family in France. After three years of correspondence, it was finally happening. My head was buzzing with questions; I was wondering how we were going to communicate with each other. We didn't speak the same language: I didn't speak French, and he did not speak Polish. But I was ready to share this man's life, a man whom I had dreamed to meet since I was very small. Even if I was happy to meet my father, I was sad because I was leaving Jacek: my brother and I did not have the same father… I felt oppressed; I felt I was abandoning my brother. Seeing him suffer from my departure, I felt so sad and so ill at ease. My heart was torn between these two males; I chose to follow my father, despite everything. To comfort myself that I'd made the right choice, I told myself that it was our only way to have a more radiant future. Leaving the orphanage, I said to Jacek, "I'm leaving for us, my brother. I promise that one day, I will come to take you."

The road to France was long and very challenging, a sixteen hours' drive, during which I tried to create a connection. My father did not speak much, because of the language barrier, and also because he was not very expressive . It was a curious feeling to be beside my father and not being able to understand him or being able to tell him how much I was happy to discover his face. We used a French-Polish dictionary to translate a few words. We were totally improvising; I tried to fill the silence with the universal language of hands. That made us laugh. The journey seemed long with all this silence and so empty without my brother. What I felt was strange, a kind of regret, a kind of guilt, too. My heart was filled with sorrow and sadness to leave, but I was also curious about the new stage of my life that was beginning.

We arrived at one o'clock in the morning. The first contact with my stepmother was very cold; she shook my hand without a smile and led me into their dark house. My new life in France, far away from my native Poland, was starting. A new language, a new culture, new food habits, a new way of communicating, everything had to start all over again. The only thing I really wanted to know was my father. I knew that it was necessary to go through this if I were to help my little brother, who had stayed at the orphanage. The first months were challenging for us all. The period of adaptation to our new life, the language barrier, and cultural differences were felt every day. When I started school, I joined a regular school schedule, like all the other children. Since I could not speak French at all, I joined a class with children three years younger than me. It was not easy for a fourteen-year-old girl to end up with eleven-year-olds. I struggled to adapt, both at home, where we did not speak and I felt a distance, and at the school, where I coped the best I could, even though I did not understand anything. The teachers were very tolerant with me, very patient. I often prayed; my only refuge was with God. I often spoke to Him in my prayers; He was my only safe home.

An Unexpected Letter

One day, my father came into my room and gave me a letter and a Franco-Polish dictionary, so I could translate what he had written to me. He immediately went out. In this letter, my father told me that he could clearly see me struggling to adapt, and I had a month to think about whether I wanted to stay with them or go back to Poland. If I decided to leave, I should forget him altogether, and he would not come back for me. This was quite a blow. I cried; I felt really lonely. I could not talk to my brother; I had no friends, and I could not call anyone in Poland, because it was too expensive for my father and stepmother. I felt a huge void inside me. I missed my brother, my friends, Poland, and my previous life. I was lost, frightened, and so disappointed that my father would not sit with me just to take me in his arms for a moment and discuss it. I started eating in secret. I ate everything I could lay my hands on: biscuits, cheese, yogurt, ice cream. I even ate at night. I would eat and then make myself throw up. I put on eight kilos in two months, and I got to such a point that I couldn't stand myself. I hated myself. I suffered from my brother's absence, my father's insensitivity towards me, and the icy atmosphere in which I lived in my new home. But I decided to stay. I knew that it was the only way for me to get through and to be able to help my brother someday.

Having the Courage to Listen to Your Heart

When I was eighteen, I fell in love with a boy I met at a music festival at which he played the saxophone. I got along very well with his parents. With my father and his wife's approval, I spent a few weekends with them. They were people of extraordinary kindness and simplicity. But when I got home, I felt tension; no one would speak to me. Television would pitifully fill the heavy silence. When I said hello, no one answered me. I hated those times; you had to pretend nothing had happened, and politely at that! I remained polite and continued to greet them. I worked hard at school, so that I would not be blamed. I had very good results, except in math. On weekends, I always did the housework to help my stepmother; I looked after my three stepbrothers. I did everything to help everyone; I did not want to disappoint, and I always avoided conflict, even to the point of being hurt. I hated that. I always felt like a stranger in that house. One day, shortly after my eighteenth birthday, my father coldly asked me to choose to either stay with them or leave the house. He told me, "You're an adult, and this house is not a hotel. You spend your time in school and doing sports, and you spend the weekend with your boyfriend. You have to make a decision, either you stay and you do what you're told, or you leave. We can no longer accept that." I felt a huge knot in my stomach. The fear had returned. I felt hurt deep inside of me. I was disoriented. I was not expecting that at all from my father, especially the year of my exams and just four years after arriving in France.

I felt such a strong tremor in my heart. With tears in my eyes, I said to my father: "I'll follow my heart, I will go where there is love, where I am finally loved for who I am. It's hard to make that choice, but I have had enough of being ignored. You've never loved me. How can you force me to choose? " I did not think about how I was going to live. I took refuge in my room, terribly hurt once again. My father did not even come talk to me. I felt abandoned again.

The next morning, it was a Sunday. My father called me and asked if I needed a hand to pack my bags. I politely replied, "No." As usual, I was polite, but inside, I felt so much pain. I felt so much fear inside of my heart. He put black 100-liter garbage bags on the stairs: they were my suitcases. I filled them, and I left the house without saying goodbye, tears in my eyes. Outside, I felt like a homeless person with my bags, I tried to be strong and to show again that I could deal with this by myself. But inside, I was ashamed and afraid. I had had the courage to make a decision without thinking about tomorrow. Even if I had to push myself further, to survive and to adapt ,this experience made me grow up a lot .

More than ever, I was motivated to pass my exams to show my father that, even without his help, I could succeed. Everyone told me I should ask him for a pension, that he had an obligation to support me. I resented him immensely for humiliating me, ignoring me, and, of course, throwing me out of the house. But deep down, I was not able to confront him in court and ask him for money. I did not want any conflict with my father; after all, I was in France thanks to him. I wanted to continue my studies, to become someone he could be proud of some day. Unknowingly, even after having been kicked out, I was trying to show him what I could do. I passed my exams with one of the three best scores in French in the region, and I passed the entrance test for a university. For two years, I took classes at that school while working at a supermarket to support myself. Despite my limited resources, I still managed to send a little money to my brother in Poland. My boyfriend's family were an invaluable support, their presence in my life was such a gift I was so grateful for all their love and presence in this challenging moment . They looked after me as if I was one of their own. Once again, I felt guided by guardian angels; there always was somebody to help me on my way.

My determination to grow did not stop there. I passed an entrance exam for a prestigious school of management in Lille. I got accepted. It was so exciting! At the same time, I got a scholarship that would allow me to pay for a small room. It was certainly not enough to live on, but I finally had my own little room, and I really was so grateful for receiving this scholarship. My boyfriend was happy to live with his parents. He was not working yet; he was an only child, and his parents were telling him to take his time. He did not understand why I wanted to study in Lille and pay for a studio flat when his parents were generously offering us their hospitality. Once again, I decided that my life did not stop at a tidy life with lunch at the same hour every day , daily visits to the grandmother's and my boyfriend playing video games every night. I was so grateful for their generosity, but inside, I felt that I did not want this life. Although I loved this family and respected them enormously, in my heart, I felt suffocated. Inside I felt guilty for this next vision of my life , This was not how I saw the rest of my life. I realized that we were not on the same wave. And it was okay. He liked stability and comfort; whereas, I was ready to move towards an unknown destination. I longed to grow and experience new things in life. So, I left him, and although it caused me a lot of pain, I knew that in order to move forward, it was necessary for him and for me to follow our own direction. Again, I was overcome by fear, but I had made my decision. So, I moved in a small studio flat in Lille on my own. I felt so alone. I wanted to show that everything was okay, but inside, I felt my heart so in pain. I started to smoke to fill the void. I was working late at night after school to pay for food and bills. I took the underground train and the bus to go to work on the other side of the town. But once I had paid the bills and had sent some money to my brother, there was nothing left until the end of the month. I was ashamed asking for money or for food. I sometimes found myself hungry, and I felt a great loneliness, but I did not regret my choice. Although I could not see the end of the tunnel, I knew that the sun always shines after the storm. In my heart, I was really dreaming that one day, everything would change, that my life would not always be like this. Despite the doubt and tears shed, I told myself that I had not come all this way to give up now. I wanted to keep the promise I had made to my brother.

Destination: Guadeloupe, the Land of Eternal Sunshine

I met love again, and it turned my life upside down. Our attraction was deep, and we were crazy in passionate love. Three months after we met, we decided to go to Guadeloupe. An opportunity presented itself to us. My boyfriend had received an offer to work in this beautiful Caribbean island.

He wanted me to go with him, and I found it touching that he made it a condition to his own departure. I therefore followed him out of love, abandoning my studies and a good job opportunity at a major retailer. Once again, I let my heart choose, and it was such a beautiful feeling!

I discovered an extraordinary country, which has now become my adopted country. Guadeloupe has been my home for 20 years now. This island, so light, with beautiful energies, sends me so much love every single day. I discovered the warmth of the Caribbean people. Its history and its impressive culture are now part of my heritage. No matter the color of our skin, I discovered a unique color of humanity : that of universal color of love. Today I am proud to be part of this family. This mixture of ethnicities, colors, and religions makes me want to savor every moment and enjoy connecting with such beautiful people. Guadeloupe is a land of beautiful waters and beautiful beaches; its nature is lush, with rivers and rainforests. Nature fills my life, it's a gift. Each new day is a blessing here.

I found work in the daily press. I was selling advertising space that made people dream. I had no experience in this domain, nor in communication. But my deep desire to work in this renowned company and especially my hunger to succeed motivated me to push myself. I could see myself in the position as if it was inevitable. I was determined, and I got the job. For four consecutive years, I made the numbers go through the roof, and soon, I tripled my salary. I felt things were finally starting to work for me. But not everything was rosy. After two-and-a-half years together, I decided to end my relationship. My partner had become jealous to excess. He found it hard to accept that I was sometimes earning more than him. He couldn't stand it when I talked to other men; his own friends were becoming a danger for him. He would make inappropriate remarks to me in public. He would even sometimes impose to change my outfit to go to work when he thought that the one I was wearing was "too low-cut". He would squeeze my wrist hard and punctuated his aggressiveness with humiliating statements. I no longer felt safe. I was afraid of him. I remembered too well my mother's suffering, and I told him that no one would touch me, not even once. But I didn't really know how to leave him. I was, once again, afraid to make a decision. And what if I was the problem? What was I once more running away from?

This was when I met Anthony, who would later become my husband. Here again, a coincidence occurred in my life. Nothing predisposed us to be together. He was not at all my type of man. But I felt good with him: he was calm and stable, and I liked our long discussions. We talked about travel, but also of our respective relationships, which brought us so much closer.

In 2001, at an airport during a trip to Paris, I came across Tony Robbins's book, *Awaken the Giant Within*. I didn't know who Tony Robbins was. The book came into my life like an invaluable gift. Tony Robbins evoked his difficult beginnings and the extraordinary method he used to transform his weaknesses into power "to live the life of his dreams". I told myself that I, too, could get there! It helped me take a new direction in my life by asking myself better questions. It definitively helped me make the decision to leave my boyfriend for Anthony. When I told him that I was leaving him for someone else, he got angry and struck me. He went after my legs and completely demolished my left tibia. I couldn't walk anymore, and I found myself unable to work. Despite this dark moment, I went through this challenging moment. I faced fear, once again.

We all are led to show courage at one time or another in our lives. Personally, I always made the best decisions when I was facing danger, when I was most scared. We all dream of having a magical life, to be happy, but our fate takes a turn when we are in action facing our fears. There is only one recipe: have the courage to face your fears! The most difficult part and what requires the most courage is the first step. This is the one step that makes all the difference. So, enjoy life, despite the fear in your stomach, and make a difference with small actions . Courage will free your energy, and you will move in new, unknown direction. If you will just allow yourself to liberate that power, everything will come in perfect time.

Today, I'm proud of my choice. It's been a long and winding road, but it doesn't matter, because I made the choice of following this inner voice, deep inside. I ardently desired it.

So, listen to your heart .The most priceless connection comes from your heart . Feel this vibrant light within your soul; don't try to hide this little voice. Choose wisely with whom you will share your energy , where you will feel safe just by being you .

Surround yourself with people who will love you not judge you , not control you, just love your presence of who you are . Choose people who will help you grow, who will challenge you, who will tell you the truth, who will just make your moments matter.

Follow your intuition; your heart already knows.

"Your time is limited, so don't waste it living someone else's life. Don't be trapped by dogma, which is living with the results of other people's thinking. Don't let the noise of others' opinions drown out your own inner voice. And most important, have the courage to follow your heart and intuition."

- Steve Jobs

Letter received from children i support in Uganda

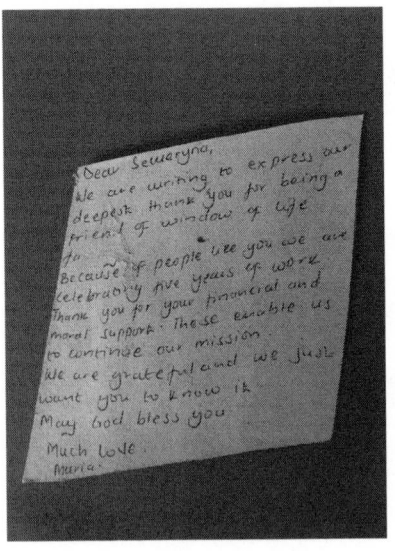

Expressing my gift

Dancing with my brother Jacek

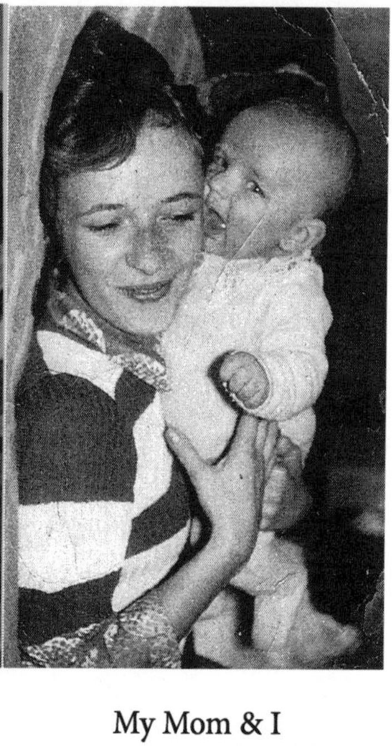

My Mom & I
I was 6 months old

My Home From My Childhood Nothing Changed Since

My Uncle Yann And My Brother

CHAPTER FIVE

Gratitude, this Power that Gives Direction to Fulfilled Life

"Gratitude unlocks the fullness of life. It turns what we have into enough, and more. It turns denial into acceptance, chaos to order, confusion to clarity. It can turn a meal into a feast, a house into a home, a stranger into a friend."

Melody Beattie

The more I age, the more I feel that my connection with life grows with me, that it becomes completely fluid. It's like a cloud that surrounds me constantly and connects my heart to everything around me.

Each day is a ritual ,and I have a feeling this bond is a gift. When I close my eyes and I put my hand on my heart, I can feel this single beat telling me that I am still here. It is marvellous to feel this life force in my heart. I like simple things: the fresh morning air, birdsong, the sour taste of the first glass of lemon water, the smell of a delicious chicory drink after a good, cold shower, the children telling me, "Mum, I love you," family breakfasts before going to school, soft music in the car, etc. These things are infinite, and they are all gifts. I am happy to be aware of it, and I do not want to lose a crumb of it, because my own happiness lies in each one of these magical moments that I have learned to enjoy over time.

I like to stop for a moment, no matter the time of day. I take a moment just for me, and I enjoy it. It is my magic moment, my daily food, which gives meaning to everything I do in life. I realize today that, since my very early childhood, I've always felt guided. I had the feeling that in all situations, even the darkest, there was always a small ray of sunshine just for me, a little shimmer to make my heart smile. Meeting certain people in your life does not come by chance. Each meeting has a meaning. This is also true for the events that dot your life.

The Guardian Angels Are Looking Out for Us.

No matter your religion, no matter what you believe in, I am certain that there is a supreme force looking out for us. We all have somebody who is predestined to cross our path at a given time of our life to make us go forward, to allow us to grow, and to give us hope in a moment of doubt. Never let us forget that we are never alone; we all are inter-connected.

Jan and His Wife

Jan and his wife were extraordinary people. I used to spend weekends at their house when I was three. We used to play a lot, and we would take walks in the park. Even though the adoption was never finalized, this extraordinary couple had a huge impact on our lives. To me, they were part of the family. Jan was like a protective father to me. Each month, he would drive across the whole region to bring a food package, so that Mum and I could live and eat properly. It was bliss in the house whenever he visited. Most of the time, it was at the end of the month, when there was no money left to buy food. He continued to help us even after my brother's birth. In my prayers, I would thank God for this food, for Uncle Jan. I was still very young, but I was old enough to feel this unconditional love that goes beyond blood ties. Not only was I fed, but Jan and his wife also gave me hope. Jan was a gift from God. Unknowingly, he was acting as a supreme force watching over us. I will never thank them enough until the day I die.

My Aunt Krystyna

My aunt Krystyna is one of those beautiful people, one of these angels sent on my path for a reason. Since I was little, she always helped my mother. Thanks to her, we had a gas cooker at home. We were so happy when it was installed. We no longer had to heat the stove to get hot water. Thanks to my aunt, I had a real First Communion ceremony with a beautiful white dress and gorgeous white sandals that someone had loaned her for the occasion. She even thought of the gift: my first watch with a red leather bracelet in a small black box. I was impatient to receive the body of Christ for the first time in my life. I felt so beautiful in church. I was like the other little girls, so pretty, with my hair done and a magnificent dress that smelled good, too. I couldn't stop sniffing my sleeves to enjoy the scent of cleanliness. Even though Krystyna lived modestly and was raising her daughter on her own, her generosity for us knew no limit. She always spent time listening to me and helping those who were in need. I liked going to her house; it smelled nice and clean. Her presence in my life is a gift.

The Kalista Family

Another gift in my life is to have met the wonderful Kalista family, who lived at the other end of the region and regularly came to the orphanage to visit the children. This very devout Catholic family of four gave their time to share their heart and their home with other children at the orphanage. One day, the Kalistas offered us to spend a weekend at their house for the holidays. My brother was all for it, but I wasn't. There were several occasions such as these before

I decided to go there at least once, because I thought they spent all their time in church, and although I was a believer myself, I could not imagine myself spending all my time praying. Mariusz, one of the four children, was the one who swayed me. He was three years my senior. He was blond with blue eyes. I liked him a lot; I do not know why. He was friendly and so helpful with everyone.

At the Kalistas', I immediately felt at home. During my first visit, they all already knew my first name. When I went there, we slept in the same room; I slept with the girls as if I were one of theirs. I was so moved by their warmth and the family atmosphere in which I was immersed that when I had to go back to the orphanage at the end of the weekend, I regretted leaving them. We would go there at least twice a month. It had become an unmissable appointment. I was happy to see that everyone adored my brother. He made everyone laugh. We had our place among them; their house was ours.

This family really taught us the values of a "united family", as well as the rules and the respect that come with it. It wasn't about blood ties, but about the heart - this family considered sharing and contribution as their core values. I am honored to have received this gift in my life. Thank you, Mariusz, for coming to the orphanage and convincing me to try at least once. Thank you for being, to this day, a model of inspiration for me. My vision of family changed completely: the more we give love to those close to us and show compassion, the more joy and happiness we receive. Thank you for all children that you helped, Mariusz, either in Poland or Uganda, in orphanages and schools. You have supported so many families and communities. Through your exemplary work, you are a brother of humanity. You are a beautiful force for good; you're an inspiration to so many people. With your big heart, your simplicity, and your discretion, you changed many lives. I honor you. I am proud to have met you. You'll always have a place in my heart.

Impacting the lives of others and contributing to their happiness is part of my mission in life thanks to you.

Signs of Ultimate Blessings

My Brother, This Force of Nature

I feel so happy to have accomplished one of the finest contributions in this world: helping Mum raise my brother, Jacek. Holding his little hand and teaching him to walk; guiding him to teach him to read and write; being at his side when he was afraid at night, when I too was afraid of the dark and Mum would leave us on our own, when he was hungry; or playing with him. I was there because I loved him, and because it had to be done. I could not leave him sad, hungry, and dirty.

Our five-year age gap was a gift, even if sometimes, it was hard to wash cloth diapers for my little brother - often by hand - when the washing machine was broken. I even had blisters on my fingers.

Sometimes, it was frustrating to see my friends playing outside with their pretty prams and dolls, whilst I, at the age of six, was peeling vegetables to feed my brother. I cannot count the number of times I heated water on the stove to prepare Jacek's evening bath in the small metal bowl. I almost burned myself many times.

Although it was often difficult, although I would sometimes cry and complain about my condition in comparison with other children, I have always found the strength in me to do what seemed right like a little girl. I don't know where it came from. This inexplicable force is present in all of us; it is something more powerful than us; a protective instinct, an instinct for survival, this guiding force for a greater good.

A sad memory comes to mind. It was May 1st. We were visiting friends of my mother's. Jacek was only four years old. We were sitting on the floor, watching cartoons on TV. We were all the more excited because our black-and-white TV had not been working for three months.

There was a good atmosphere: bottles of vodka on the table, and everyone had already been drinking quite a lot. During the evening, Mum's friend tripped on the couch, flipping over a kettle of hot water, intended to infuse tea, over my brother.

It was a real nightmare! Jacek started to scream in pain. His pain was cruel. His arm, his chest, and his leg were burnt. His skin was melting into his blue wool sweater. Mum was so drunk that she could not even move off her chair. I didn't have time to think; I had to take care of Jacek. I had to take off his sweater, which was melting into his wounds. The skin was open; I could see his bloodied flesh. Mum's friend told me that I had to pour cold water on first, then milk, to attenuate the pain. I managed to take his jumper off that by then had stuck to his skin. Jacek's suffering was horrendous. I didn't know how to soothe him. I cried and had pains in my stomach. I didn't sleep a wink all night, so I could watch my brother. I feared that something would happen if I fell asleep. All night, I changed the towels I used as bandages. I would soak them first in cold water, and then, in milk. I delicately applied them to the open wounds. The process made me feel nauseated. Nobody was able to drive my brother to the hospital: all the adults were in a state of intoxication, and with hindsight, I wonder whether they realized what state my brother was in. It was night-time, we did not have a car, and, of course, we did not have money to take a taxi. Someone said, "Tomorrow, we will have to go and see the doctor." That night was one longest in my life. Jacek had a high fever and was shivering. I felt impotent. All I could do was stay by his side. He didn't want me to leave him; he would lay his other hand on me to check if I was still beside him. I was so scared for him. The next morning, we got on a bus to the doctor's. Jacek was exhausted; he still had a high fever. Despite everything, he managed to walk. I was proud; he was so brave! I wonder still today where he drew this force from. The doctor observed with fascination this thin little boy who stood valiantly, in spite of his deep burns. The doctor was astonished that with such wounds, we had not gone to the hospital earlier. He looked at my mother. She had tears in her eyes. He looked at me and said, "You did the right thing by taking off his wool sweater and cooling his wounds. If you had not done it, he would be in a more serious state." Mum felt guilty; I saw her eyes filled with tears and compassion for her little boy. I shivered. I wanted to vomit, as if I continuously felt my brother's physical suffering. I was so very disappointed in my mother. At that moment, I was ashamed to be her daughter; I felt in the doctor's glance all the contempt that she inspired in him. I could not say that she had been drunk and that it was the reason why we had arrived so late. And yet, I wanted only one thing at that moment: to pour my anger over her.

Thank you, God, for guiding me in these moments, to have allowed me to assist my little brother, to have helped me do it with patience and compassion, the best that I could.

A Miracle: My Brother is Alive

When Jacek was twelve years old, I almost lost him. I was not told about it, and I was far away from him. He had terrible pains in his stomach and began coughing up blood. Without anyone's help, he climbed the hill to the hospital. He stopped several times along the way; he was exhausted. At the hospital, the doctors took him to the emergency room: he had ulcers, and they had burst in his stomach. The bleeding was so great, he was operated on in an emergency. A few days after the operation, he had lost a lot of weight and was getting worse. He was diagnosed with a general infection: it was septicaemia. He was operated on a second time in an emergency. The doctors were not giving up; they tried everything. Despite the electroshocks, his heart stopped. Then, there was a miracle! A first heartbeat appeared on the screen after five minutes of clinical death. My brother came back to life. Later, he told me with a smile and a kind of inner peace, that he had seen his body from above. He was lying on the operating table, surrounded by doctors. He felt attracted by an almost palpable white light and felt like he was being sucked into a tunnel, but gradually the white light subsided, and he heard voices. They were the doctors' voices. How can this miracle be explained?

I tell myself that there is nothing to explain, that there are forces more powerful than us guiding us throughout our lives.

No one had told me that he was in hospital; I didn't know about his critical condition, nor his clinical death. Once my brother recovered, about three weeks after the operation, I received a letter from him. He wanted to reassure me. When I read it, I was devastated. Our mother had only visited him well after his operations. I was heartbroken when I told my father what had happened. I told him about my wish to pay him a visit. Since my brother was better and I was soon to be eighteen years old, he forced to me to wait! My father had my passport, and I had no money, so I could not do anything. I was so angry with him. I was also angry with my mother for not having been at my little brother's side. I felt anger, sadness, and disappointment. However, I was relieved—and especially grateful—that my brother was alive. I took the telephone and called the hospital. I talked to a nurse, an exceptional woman, who already knew who I was. She told me everything in an emotional voice. She said that it was a miracle that Jacek was alive: the day before his operation, the priest had even come to give him his last rites, since he was so weakened and thin. She added that she liked my brother very much, that he was determined to live, that he was smiling; he was, in fact, the ray of sunshine in the service. Then, she handed the phone over to Jacek. When I heard his sweet voice, I was reassured, and I cried with joy. He shared with me his magical moment in the beyond. He was happy to be back and to have experienced this sensation. I listened to him, filled with love; I drank his words filled with the joy of living. I was terribly angry with myself for not being there when he had needed me the most. I felt like a coward for not standing up to my father.

This powerlessness made me sad, I locked myself up for one day in my room upstairs. I was not well; I completely cracked up. I sat on the floor, leaning against my bed, and I took out a razor blade I had stolen from my father. I felt completely out of control. I lay the blade against my arm, and I clenched my teeth. When I was just about to let the blade cut through my veins, I heard a noise in the staircase. I stopped. Then, after a silence, I heard a voice in my head whispering, *Do not do it, he needs you.* I broke down in tears on the floor. I took a cushion and howled into it with all my strength, so that nobody could hear me. I was exhausted and felt like I was hallucinating. I lay down in a ball and fell asleep like a baby. When I woke up, it was almost dark outside. I felt like I had lived through a nightmare. I couldn't believe that I could lose control of myself. I realized how much I was hurting inside and how my soul was crying for help. But I was safe. I thanked God for stopping me in time. I felt so ashamed to have selfishly thought of myself and my state of mind, instead of focusing on how I could support my brother. I immediately started writing to him, my heart at peace and filled with gratitude and love for him.

Thanks to that moment, I know that nothing is more valuable than the smile of the people I love.

Second Chance

On November 7th, 2009, three days after our mum's death, as I embarked from Paris to Guadeloupe, my brother left Poland. He, too, had to travel to meet his family in Guadeloupe. We were not booked on the same flight.

He was on the motorway when he was taken with a violent nausea. He started vomiting blood. The driver of the vehicle managed to get to the nearest hospital just before Jacek lost consciousness. The operation lasted more than eight hours. The doctors couldn't find the origin of the bleeding in his stomach. Each minute was crucial. He had to have a blood transfusion, as he was losing too much blood. At that time, I was on the aircraft and had no idea what was going on. However, at one time, suddenly, I gasped for air, and I started having palpitations. I was cold and felt terribly distressed. Without knowing why, I had the intuition that something was wrong; then, I lost consciousness. I later found out it was a vasovagal episode. I spent the rest of the trip with an oxygen mask on.

Anthony came to greet me at the airport. I told him what had happened on the plane. My husband knew what had happened to Jacek, but he decided to wait until I got home to tell me. When he finally told me what had happened, I shivered. I was devastated. Once again, I was not near my brother when he was going through a difficult time. After what seemed like an endless wait, we received a call: the bleeding had stopped after eight hours, and the operation had been a success. It was a new miracle, because the ulcer he had been suffering from was tiny and almost impossible to spot. The most extraordinary thing in this story is that the bleeding started before he boarded the plane. As well as this, the hospital that took care of him, without him choosing it, specialized in gastric disorders. Once again, the guardian angels were looking after Jacek on that day.

The Greatest Miracle: Signs of a Rebirth

My brother, Jacek, married Kasia, a Polish lady, an amazing woman, and they have two adorable children aged three and six. Their son, Evan, is a pure miracle. Indeed, the most beautiful day in the lives of my brother and my sister-in-law should have been the arrival of their first child, Evan. It was on September 16ᵗʰ , 2009. We were all very excited to see their little angel for the first time. But this blessed day almost turned into nightmare: Evan came to the world, but he was purple and remained inert. What dreadful sorrow. Doctors and midwives tried in vain to revive him. The life of this little angel was in their hands. After five long, endless minutes, his little heart started to beat. There was no intensive care service in the clinic where Evan was born and no spaces at the nearest hospital, so a helicopter took the baby to a hospital on the other end of the island, away from his mother. Suffice to say that there was no time to lose. Jacek, in tears and utter shock, drove to the intensive care unit, where his son had been admitted in Basse-Terre. He drove across the whole of Guadeloupe in record time, just to be near his baby. During the helicopter ride, the doctors had to, once again, rescue the little boy whose heart had stopped again. A new miracle happened! Our little angel was coming back to life. Just like his father, Evan survived.

In moments like these, you don't ask yourself, "What shall I do, how can I do it?" You do what you have to do, and that's it. Saving a human life is a wonderful gift. What a blessing it is to see little Evan come back to life and be the joy of the family today! Just for this, I'm full of gratitude for all these miracles that take place every day; they amaze me every time I think about them.

My Dearest Dream Becomes Reality

One day, my brother came to visit me in Guadeloupe—I had gotten him a ticket. We were so happy to be together again! He still had one year of studies in Poland, and he had to take his exams to graduate. I told him, "If you pass your exams, you can come to live in Guadeloupe with me. I would be always there for you!" My brother is very strong; each day, I admire his courage and his unshakable faith. Indeed, this young lad had to have courage to overcome the orphanage, drugs, cigarettes, and alcoholism. His close friends regularly used these. He sometimes found himself in situations where he could have sunk. He told me that he was able to hang on, because I was there to show him the way. I was his inspiration.

He was determined to change his life journey and to come to live in Guadeloupe with me. This deep desire of living an extraordinary life became reality after several challenging years. I am so grateful for this gift of resiliency .

My brother has now been living in Guadeloupe for eighteen years with his family, near me. We appreciate these priceless moments that are offered to us today . This experience was somewhat challenging in the beginning, because of the cultural differences and the language barrier. But thanks to the support given by Anthony, Jacek created his own company! Today, he renovates houses, allowing people to make their dreams reality. Nothing makes me happier today than seeing my dearest dream finally come true. No matter how long it took, my brother lives with me, and he is in excellent health, surrounded by a loving family. Nothing is more important than seeing the happiness in the eyes of those we love most in the world. A simple smile on Jacek's face is enough to make me feel happy and full of gratitude.

Having the courage to go after your dreams allows you to rise, gives you the ability to expand yourself, and to change the lives of others around you.

These challenges have taught me how fragile and beautiful life is at one and the same time. Life is gifted to us in every moment. We don't know how long the trip will last, nor how many trump cards we will have. The only thing that matters is living in the present moment and being grateful, because everything is a gift. What's I learned for sure is that we can't control what happening outside—the only one thing we can control is just the meaning we give to each situation we are experiencing .

Life is the experience of an eternal renewal filled with miracles. Sometimes, in just a second, a decision is enough to save the life of one human being. So, let's use our presence every day in our small daily acts of kindness.

So, today and even more after all these storms in my life, I am just grateful for each of them, for never giving up, even if sometimes, I really wanted to finish it all. Just feeling how much humans' lives has been touched by my own way of courageously experiencing all these chapters, which helps me find a new meaning and my passion for helping others to find hope in their own journey .

Feeling peace now is allowing myself to open my heart to receive and to give freely this   wave of love and compassion around me and smiling to each tiny gift of life,

Connecting to my soul, it's just vibrating life, itself, just now .... just now.

PRESENCE: this is who I am.

COURAGE: this is what I do each and every day.

FEAR : this is what I went through and still go through so many times to finally realize that it's my call to action .

LOVE : this is ME since I was born; I just forgot it for a while. My mission today is to share with simplicity that tiny sparkle of love around me , because each life touched by lovely caring matters .

"What I receive I must pass on to others. The knowledge that I have acquired must not remain imprisoned in my brain. I owe it to many men and women to do something with it. I feel the need to pay back what was given to me. Call it gratitude."

- Elie Wiesel

CHAPTER SIX

The Power of Continuous Learning

"Obstacles don't have to stop you. If you turn into a wall, don't turn around and give up. Figure out how to climb it, go through it, or work around it."

Michael Jordan

Learning is what makes us free and happy. This thirst for constant self-improvement and knowledge of the world around us opens the door to extraordinary horizons. The more you have access to knowledge, the more you are able to choose, to decide what is best for you. Never stop learning—it is the only way to grow and "achieve the impossible". This is the only gift we can carry everywhere with us. This is what keeps us alive. This is the real progress.

I want to share my amazing journey during which I became aware of my real purpose in life and allowed me to become a better person. This is my greatest asset, and it thrills me every day.

Getting Out of Your Comfort Zone

I remember the day when Anthony came to me and said, "Time has come for you to go for it." At first, I didn't understand what he meant. Then, I remembered mentioning to him two years earlier that my greatest dream was to be part of the prestigious Platinum Partner family, an extraordinary life experience at Tony Robbins's side. He offered me a trip to *Business Mastery* in London in 2014.

I remember the fear I felt at the time. I came to realize that my English wasn't good enough to be trained exclusively in English. I wondered how I would understand without translation this man who inspired me so much. Some tried to discourage me: "How will you manage? There are no translators, you will not manage; it's too hard. If I were you, I would not go—it's too expensive for what you'll learn." Various thoughts began to overcome me. Fear began to take over. I wondered how we would manage financially. I felt guilty. I thought I was being a bit selfish, thinking of all the hard-earned savings I was going to spend. I didn't want to deprive my family of holidays for a training that might serve only me. Then, I closed my eyes for a moment, away from all the noise that was disturbing my mind. For a moment, I connected to my heart. I realized that all this did was not happening by chance, and it was a gift that the Universe was sending me for a reason. I could already visualize how this progress would allow my whole family to grow. I didn't yet know how dramatically I was going to progress, nor did I know how my change would influence my loved ones around me. I was sure of one thing: I had to go—it was my destiny. Another chapter of my life was decided at this moment. I created it in my mind, in my prayers, and the Universe presented me the opportunity to rub shoulders with Tony Robbins. I would learn the success strategies from the best experts, and I would be part of an incredible family of talented people from all over the world, who dared to dream bigger, despite their fears and hardships.

My desire to learn from the best in the world and to help my family was stronger than anything. I had no choice but to find a quick way to learn English and thereby understand Tony. I promised myself that I'd do anything for it. I said nothing of all these fears to my husband—or to anyone, for that matter. Once again, I had to make a firm decision. I signed the contract to take part in the Platinum Mastermind. I was going to attend at all costs, even if I did not speak English. Today, I am so grateful and so proud to have accomplished my dreams, to have faced this new challenge.

During that enriching year, I was constantly put to the test. This constant necessity to adapt, the flexibility and deep desire to go further and higher were of great help during my learning. I used my creativity to connect with people around the world. Despite our cultural and linguistic differences, we were all going in the same direction; we wanted to become better versions of ourselves . It was so beautiful to see all these people coming from this place of serving and love. I learned that, to be successful in life, you had to have a ritual and daily discipline: taking care of my body, my mind, and my nutrition became my first priority. My body is a temple and reflects the expression of my soul. The more I looked after cultivating my inner garden, the more flourishing my outdoor garden was. I realized that the difference lies in the little details. I absorbed valuable lessons, and I watched everything that was happening around me. With admiration, I learned to accept the differences that make the world richer.

Let me share with you two of the life-changing trips that were essential in my journey of becoming the woman I became and still become each and every day .

Spiritual Journey in India –

The Beauty of Awakening to the Present Moment.

Spiritual journey in India, seminar with Tony Robbins - Oneness Temple and the magic of the Ganges.

Sometimes, you need to lose yourself to be able to find the courage to free your soul and to create this new version of you . When you don't know what to do, you are in this perfect state of surrender, your senses are open to be guided. You don't know why, but you feel different, your senses are awakened, and your perception is sharpened. Something new awaits you at every turn, and your brain is alert, detecting every new detail. And what better place than India to completely find a new version of self?

In 2014, I travelled to India for my first spiritual seminar. This trip was one of the most profound journeys of my life. From the beginning, good fortune smiled at me. Two days before my trip, I received an email upgrade. My first flight to Dubai would be in business class. I could not believe it; I was going to join Tony Robbins and his platinum mastermind family in India, sitting comfortably for the first time in my life in business class. I was like a little girl feeling so excited and so grateful. This adventure to the other side of the globe opened my eyes to the beauty of human nature. There, for the first time, I felt in perfect connection with all humans I crossed during the trip. While I didn't speak English, I could make myself understood through gestures and facial expressions. There was a lot of beautiful laughter! The Hindus had a profound effect on me. Their eyes glowed with a spark of joy, the joy of the present moment. They had nothing, and for some, they survived on the streets and were dressed in just a piece of fabric. The lack of attachment to material things made these people so rich. They offered me one of the most beautiful lessons of life perception. I felt as never before, deep inside me, the meaning of the terms of "the present moment", "living in simplicity", and "stop complaining". Several times a day, I felt moments of profound gratitude. I understood how lucky I was to live in a free and wealthy country.

In India, I lived through one of the most extraordinary spiritual experiences. I attended teachings, followed by meditation in one of the largest temples in southern India: Oneness Temple. What a privilege to have been able to meditate in such a sacred place! I felt new sensations throughout my body. A kind of trance came over me; I felt a kind of detachment from my own body. Under my eyelids, a spectrum of colors turned into a kaleidoscope. Circles were forming and disappearing to make room for new colored forms. As the experience progressed, a yellow and white light filled the space around me. I was conscious, I did not want to open my eyes because it was so beautiful, and I wanted to carry on enjoying the moment. Suddenly, an electric shock went through my body, and I felt a tapping sensation on my back. Extreme heat radiated from my hands. I felt as if my limbs were moving on their own. I was aware of all those feelings that my body was experiencing, and it was divine. I felt like electric dust, like a free electron in full appreciation of a unique experience.

Within this unique place, I realized that each of us is part of a single whole; here, they call it "ONENESS". The energy that each of us creates releases vibrations and form a single "ONE" being part of all.

The day following this memorable day, another wonderful surprise awaited us. A private jet took us from Chennai to Varanasi. It was like a fairy tale. On arrival, we boarded a bus that took us to a beautiful palace in Chennai. A princely welcome awaited us. After lunch, we went to Tony Robbins and his sweet wife, Sage, and we got into barges. All the boats had been carefully decorated with beautiful flowers. This evening ride on the Ganges, with the rhythmic sound of paddles, was full of mystery. The beauty of this civilization was present in this sacred moment. On that barge, I felt like the energy of ancient souls were all around me. Finally, each of us received a candle in a basket of flowers. The tradition was to place the basket on the water and think of our most precious dream. The next day, at dawn, we returned to this history-filled place to admire the sunrise and watch the traditional bathing in the Ganges. I remember perfectly the mixture of bright colors, beautiful fabrics, the painted faces of people who were meditating, and the men who purified themselves in the river. On the edge of the river, we could see women dressed in long, colorful dresses, with their hair carefully done up, who sold souvenirs. Some wore beautiful necklaces adorned with orange flowers. It was a unique spectacle.

A new tour on the Ganges was awaiting us that morning. This time, we would admire the traditional Hindu bathing in the holy river at sunrise. Once again, a magical emotion went through my body. I felt a sort of tingling in my back and my arms, and a desire to cry for joy enveloped me. It was as if I could feel the energy of the souls of ancient Hindus, whose ashes had been scattered in the river.

Every day, before long hours of lessons with world-renowned experts, we started our days at 6 a.m. with a yoga session taught by the famous Guru Singh. I didn't know this old man before that visit. I still remember his blue eyes, his long white beard, but especially his passion for music and the wisdom that emanated from him. Every day, he took us to distant horizons through his kindness , and his songs filled with messages of peace and love. Sitting on the floor, he played the guitar, gently swaying his body. I had tears in my eyes. Guru Singh was present and kind with everyone. His graceful presence was just so calming and inspiring. You could read the wisdom of time on his face.

To top it all, Tony taught us every day, with passion and energy, the precious keys to mindfulness. I did not understand everything, but I sat there, attentive to the vibrations of his body and the intonation of his voice: I didn't want to miss anything—every moment was sacred. This total immersion and this hunger to learn enabled me to experience one of the most powerful points of nonverbal communication. What an incredible gift it was to experience this connection by focusing exclusively on my energy and my senses. It turned out that by connecting myself with all the other senses aside from language, I discovered other sensations. I was absorbed by everything that was happening in the room; it was like a dream. Sometimes, I would even dismiss my need to go to the bathroom, so I wouldn't miss anything of what was going on! Tony's powerful energy, his voice, his physiology, his eyes, allowed me to connect to the deeper meaning of his message. I was absorbed by all that surrounded me, free of the weight of the words and their meaning. I was in the present moment, as if I were in a dream.

I was surprised to discover the capacity a human being has to adapt in all circumstances and use all of his senses to bind deeply with his kind. Here is a noble and beautiful lesson: no matter the culture, the language, the religion, the emotional heart-to-heart connection is the key to open the doors to love and compassion.

This day will forever remain engraved in my memory.

After another intense day of seminars, Tony asked questions to the people in the room about their experiences. I raised my hand. My heart was beating fast, but I was determined to speak to Tony. I couldn't go back; he had seen me. He told me, "Please, I'm listening." Suddenly, there was a great silence in the room, and hundreds of eyes turned to me. Then, the fear disappeared and gave way to gratitude, to the appreciation of the present moment. Once again, I noticed that with faith, the impossible becomes possible. I started talking. Both fragile and determined, I heard myself speak English with great ease. More than ever, I felt that I was ready to give myself away, to open my heart, to share my joy of living.

Fifteen years after I had read his book, I was there, facing my mentor, in India, in a sacred place, and I was speaking English to tell him of my respect and my gratitude . An extraordinary connection between our hearts occurred, in this magical place forever. I felt how much this man had appreciated my courageous presence .

He was there, in front of me, his heart filled with immense love for humanity. His simplicity and his sincere smile moved me deeply. I wasn't scared anymore; I was there, connected to his heart. I just wanted to say thank you, to express my deep gratitude for what he had accomplished in this world for so many people. I would have liked to tell him so much more, but I nonetheless felt my linguistic limitations.

It was such a moving moment—my body was speaking all by itself, there was no resistance, and all the people in the room were applauding. I felt like a blessing, an abundance of love offered to me in that moment. It was a moment of perfect alignment, we were at "One" in this moment of universal joy.

Trip to Australia - The Power of Synchronicity

I remember this splendid journey perfectly. I was about to attend the famous Tony Robbins seminar, *Date with Destiny*, on relationships. I could not have missed the opportunity to spend time in my mentor's company, all the more so in Australia! But I very nearly missed it. After a long flight from Guadeloupe to Paris, I went to the counter to check in for Australia. Two hours before take-off, I was told that I needed a visa to go there. The quickest way to obtain one took seventy-two hours, and I had to go to the embassy. My eyes filled with tears, I looked at the stewardess at the counter and explained the purpose of my trip and what it meant to me. She looked at me and said, "Give me your documents, I'll see what I can do with my manager. I can't promise you anything." The wait seemed endless, but I stayed calm. There was no other way for me other than to go; I couldn't conceive otherwise. At one point, I got scared. I closed my eyes and told myself, "God, only You can decide if I should go or not. Everything is in Your hands. Then, You will choose what is best for me." I thought I hadn't come all this way just to turn back!

The woman came back with a smile on her face . I felt her message before she started to talk; "You're so lucky. I was able to get you a visa. Next time, do what you need before you leave." I couldn't believe it; my heart was just full of gratitude and my eyes full of tears of joy! I took the stewardess in my arms, held her tight, and thanked her from the bottom of the heart. Again, I felt I had been guided. I just closed my eyes and deeply thanked God for this next beautiful gift. Once I had checked in, I went to a shop to buy her a box of chocolates. She was so happy and just told me, "You have such a beautiful energy. I really wanted to help you. I felt your honesty and your excitement to go on this trip. I had no words; everything was just perfectly aligned and manifested at the right time without effort. I realized again that for those who truly believe and have fajth, the divine source provides us everything we need in perfect timing. I just experienced how the law of attraction works.

In fact, the idea to write my first book really came to life during the seminar, in which I met Chris Weaver. Chris is a Platinum member of Tony Robbins's team... and, coincidentally, an Australian publisher! I met him thanks to my friend, Shirley. While I was telling her about my dream of writing my book to help women and children in the world believe in themselves , she said, "Here, it's funny, because tonight, Chris will be there. He's a friend, and he is a publisher. I'll introduce you to him if we are lucky enough to see him today." Later in the evening, I was waiting for Shirley and, while the room was crowded, I exchanged glances with a man. He came towards me and we started talking. Then, Shirley arrived. With a smile on her lips, she said, "You already know Chris?" Isn't it incredible? Shirley told him about my dream of writing a book, and Chris said that he'd like to hear my story. He then offered to meet the following day. I went to his office on the seafront. I told him my story in English, the best I could. It was quite a challenge, but I did it, and I managed, because I saw on his face that my story had moved him. He immediately believed in my project and gave me a few tips on how to write and organize my project.

This trip to Australia is for me a beautiful symbol of synchronicity. There is always somebody who can give you a hand or show you the way if your dream supports more lives. We meet people who are like magnets, and we attract what we think about. So, we need to be careful what we think about on a daily basis . This magnetism still works today, I'm sure.

Sometimes, you need to go to the other side of the earth to realize that you already have everything inside of you to live your mission now. Sometimes, it takes time and courage to hear this inner voice of the heart. You need to take a long path of learning to finally enjoy the beauty and simplicity of this voice of your purpose here .

"Don't dismiss the synchronicity of what is happening right now finding its way to your life at just this moment. There are no coincidences in the Universe, only convergences of will, intent, and experience."

- Neale Donald Walsch

CHAPTER SEVEN

Awakening to the Infinite Feminine Power

"Once you give yourself permission to enjoy more time expressing your purpose and following your true joy, it becomes addictive, and you just want more of it."
Kimberley Jones

The Plenitude of a Fulfilled Woman...the Journey from Fear to Self-love

I discovered something important, a passion for life, this real purpose, which I have for so long underestimated the power. I was always asked myself, "You have to discover your passion , what do you really like to do?" What could it be? How do you choose your passion? I didn't really know how to do this. I remember I told myself: I don't have time between work, children, and the house! I do not paint, I do not play a musical instrument. Yes, I do love reading and dancing. I like to enjoy the various pleasures in life: swimming, running, walking through nature, meditating by the sea, devouring a good book while drinking herbal tea, going to see a movie with the children, or spending time with a friend enjoying a glass of red wine.

Gradually, as my search went on, I noticed a transformation happening inside me. The more I began to be myself, the more I respected my inner rhythm, the more I felt an inner peace. What I am very happy about is to be aware of what I experience in my daily life: breathing fresh air in the morning, eating healthily, watching my children run, enjoying the smile of an old lady at the local market, marvelling at every little sign of life.

Sometimes, when I feel a little under the weather and my energy is down, or when a challenge arises, I shake myself up, or I think of something I am grateful for , and pleasant memories fill my mind and my body. I discovered that my physical condition had a huge influence on how I felt. When a storm comes into my head, I think: "Accept, observe, and let go. You have the right to experience these emotions; it's just you. You're learning something from that experience."

Each connection to what surrounds me in this world has a meaning. Whether it's a connection to others, to myself, or to God. The more I unveil myself, the more I receive and the more fluid and simple everything becomes. The fewer questions I ask, the more I become sensitive to the signs my heart sends. Everything spontaneously aligns, because everything resonates inside me.

I'm so grateful to finally discover that being vulnerable is an extraordinary force. I no longer feel shame and guilt. On the contrary, it is with kindness and compassion that I look at my past, at the person I have become. I want to continue to learn and do my best; that's how I embrace each experience. I feel free and alive.

I feel that today, I am on my own path. I have finally understood the true meaning of passion residing in each moment: simply enjoying the present moment and learning how to grow through challenges. I am pleased to have found a passionate woman inside me. I feel this energy in every cell of my body. It is embodied in either a tear of happiness or a tingling in my body, through a feeling of lightness or a smile. These physical signs make me feel that my heart and my body are connected with life, itself, that I am just one with this moment.

I am so grateful to be this girl who marvels at the beauty of a small ladybug, dances in the rain, or admires the bird singing on the terrace... I enjoy my existence and this life that is always there for teaching me something today.

That is my definition of success!!!

Do not be afraid to dream big—life is full of surprises. Don't be afraid to fail. You will become stronger. Don't be ashamed to express your voice—only you have the power to bring your unique gift to this world with your truth, with your expression of your authentic self .

This is the magic that happens in all its splendor. Lose yourself in this dance, and let yourself explore this dark and light side of your journey. Sometimes, it's hard. There are periods of questioning, disconnection, and sadness, but it always gets back on track. Your life takes a different form every day. You just need to show consistency for yourself and commitment to your dreams and, above all, have faith. Every day, you can feel whether you are approaching your goal or if you moving away from it. You are continuously challenged, but thanks to these challenges, you become resilient in the middle of the chaos, and you find the courage to move forward. Your deepest faith will always guide your destiny . You are guided always.

Without my life's challenges, I would not be where I am today, writing this book. Yet I cannot write; in any case, that's what I thought until I started. I don't know how to do it, but I'm just trying my best, because I cannot keep all this just for me. I realized it's not about me anymore, that there is probably another person in this world who feels lost today and needs some help to believe in her worth, to believe again that there is always a new way to start again .

Giving the best of you each day, being yourself, and accepting your imperfections are the most authentic gifts you have to offer during your lifetime. Be real—you have nothing to prove, nothing to hide; you have only this life to express your truth. And by doing that, you will be able enjoy the process and to impact someone else's life. Yes, you are enough the way you are.

I let my hand run over this keyboard, my eyes fill with tears of joy, I feel excited to share with you the journey of my life. I feel a huge emotion. I feel swept away by the energy in my body. You can do the same. Take this step further today: let your heart speak. This sharing in these few sheets of paper will forever immortalize the connection to your heart, to your truth . What matters to me now is that I did it. I learned something important, perhaps the most important thing in my life: our story may influence a person's life who is lost and needs help today; you never know whose life you will transform just because of your courage to be seen the way you truly are. Giving hope, helping change the life of a child, a mother, a father, forever is the real destiny for every one of us. So, wake up to your life, give yourself the gift to reach the highest branches. Do not settle for less— strive for excellence, and be patient. Live life to the fullest, enjoy the process, and be bold. Only you can change your path, create the new story of your life, the story you want to live now. Just know one thing: time does not exist; it is just an illusion. What counts is the emotion of this moment and the energy we put into what we do. Live life to the fullest—yesterday is already over, tomorrow is not yet, and today, it's time to act . And just surrender the process.

Every time you feel this discomfort, try just for one moment to connect with what scares you the most. All these emotions of fear, shame, disappointment, and anger are part of your essence, my dear, and this is exactly where all shifts start. They increase your strength. Don't reject them anymore—they are your internal clock, listen to them, they have so much to tell you.

They constantly guides you to your truth . The more you reject them, the more you resist and so, you disconnect yourself from what is most mysterious in you, your radiant flow of your soul, your purest voice of who you truly are.

Your vulnerability is your wisdom; it's your magical power. Dare to be you—you have so much to give from this place of authenticity. Own your glow, be whole, be YOU in this chaos. .....

FROM FEAR TO LOVE

"With integrity you have nothing to fear, since you have nothing to hide. With integrity, you will do the right thing, so you will have no guilt." - Zig Ziglar

Courage to stand for something more: standing for love beyond fear.

Have you ever had the feeling that everything in your life is doing so well, but inside, you have this inner knowing there is a part of you which deeply knows that there is something you're holding on for so long, and only you know it and you keep convincing yourself that there is just a thinking, and you continue to avoid to see the truth of your real you?

How many obstacles I have already overcome in my life and how many decisions I have taken were not only the best ones, but ones that helped me grow from my mistakes.

I didn't expect there would be another level, nor one that would be so painful. I realized it was still this hidden fear within which made me diminish my inner spark .This resistance was preventing my soul from expressing my full potential, the core of my authentic essence.

It takes courage to tell the truth; when you know you will hurt someone, not only one person, but one family. It takes this bravery to tell the truth in the name of love, of integrity, in the name of the higher good. Before taking this step to speak my truth, I cried so much in silence, doubting myself, asking myself if it was the right decision. But this inner feeling never lies: it was the moment to become a woman who owns her voice, who felt her inner calling expanding within. It was a moment to stand for me for what I deserve: my fulfillment.

After 16 years of living together, I told my husband I was going to leave him. I felt so guilty about how this could impact our children's lives, their well-being: this family, this treasure I cherished the most in my life. When I told him, I saw his face. He was lost. I felt so much pain for him. I asked God to give me this strength and the right words to express my truth with compassion, and love. I felt it was the right moment. I felt guided. I wanted to leave this relationship with respect for his soul; no one deserves to be hurt.

It was harder to stay in that place of silence and hiding myself than make a decision to be seen just for who I am and to be courageous and honest for both of us.

I realize how much I avoided connecting with this uncomfortable feeling within. I did things the best I could to make everyone happy, to serve my family, my children, to serve and honor my husband who worked hard for us, to create a beautiful life we lived in our home sweet home, and it made me happy—of course, I was so grateful for everything we created together. At the same time, I felt alone with my dreams, with my desires, inside of my heart. I did not feel understood, and sometimes, I felt like my vision was not a "real thing" for him, that I totally understood with time.

I felt there was never enough of what I could do; something was always not done yet or something was missing .So I often asked myself, *Did I do something wrong?* So, I didn't feel safe to share my feelings anymore. I sometimes felt like I was not myself. I couldn't be completely "nake" with my real emotion in his presence. It was like hiding one part of me to avoid some conflicts, this pattern I unconsciously repeated from my childhood.

So, I felt his pain and pain for myself not being congruent to him. So, it was time to stop hurting him by being selfish and not telling him the truth. It was also time to stop beating myself and just be my truest self. I realized that the most respectful way of loving his soul and respecting and honoring his presence was by telling him the truth and leaving this relationship with integrity and love. It was not about him anymore; it was about honoring and embracing my own way of living my life, my choice of living in alignment with my heart's desires.

Telling my truth not only liberated my soul, but above all, I felt it was the most congruent way to respect his way of being him, respecting where he is in his life journey and honoring this man and his needs for that. He doesn't deserve to be hurt. He just wanted the best for our family, and he always did the best he could. I will be forever grateful.

So, instead of judging or blaming what I used to do in the past, I started to take responsibility for my own choices, taking new decisions and courage to tell the truth . I wanted to heal that part of me, to discover who I am in my core, what I had to let go to free myself from this last resistance and to find my last fulfillment.

I realized it's time to step into this uncertainty, into the unknown . It was scary to face my own shadows. It was time to discover who I truly am by spending time in my emotional home, taking time for loving myself and celebrating this vulnerable woman, beyond that mask, this filter that protected me from my real feelings.

The truth is that I was afraid of feeling my own rising desire of standing for something more for myself. I wanted just to express my authentic self, my joy of living, my scars, my passion for growing and using my gift to serve others .The most precious thing for me was expressing my authentic voice without feeling judged or controlled .

This beautiful family we created provided me this safety, this love I had been craving since I was young. I felt so blessed and really happy with my life where I was, but one part of my soul was craving for something deeper: this level of soul connection, this mysterious chemistry just by looking in each other's eyes without any words , this caring touch, this playfulness, this deep level of trust, time of simple presence and appreciation of little things, time to laugh together, time for being me with all my scars and my shadows.

I realized again I was looking in depth of the eyes of fear, but this time, I was embracing her darkness, experiencing her sadness . Feeling her power in that moment was just so liberating. This moment of letting go of control and just being present with this feeling allowed me access to this deepest level of compassion for another human being. It was another precious gift in my life journey to learn to use this energy of fear in service of love, instead of using fear to paralyze me, to pull me down. Yes, it felt scary at the beginning, and it was new for me, but this uncomfortable feeling started to dissolve, and this compassion for myself started to rise up. I felt at home, at peace with my soul.

We can still love and respect someone without living in the same home anymore, because there is no separation, there is just a different way of living life. It was not the end of something; it was the beauty of a new beginning for each of us.

The meaning we give to each life experience gives us the quality of choice, and each choice based on fear or love determines the quality of our relationships and automatically the different vibration of life we are going to live.

Only love wins, nothing else. Love, respect, and compassion, and only in this dimension, there is no fear anymore, there is just compassion, there is joy in simple moments of growth and new becoming .

The most important to me is being brave enough by being an example of honesty for myself first . Choosing integrity is the best way of being an example for our children who watched us. Showing them the beauty of imperfection by being a human being, making mistakes, and learning from them. What I value the most is always doing what's right, even if nobody is watching: this is being honest and aligned with humanity's highest values: love and integrity. And we have to start doing that with ourselves first. If we don't respect ourselves, no one will . This is how I learned to set my own boundaries.

All these lessons helped me discover this woman I was born to be—not a perfect one, but a real one. So grateful for this journey.

" Without darkness, there is no light. Embrace both of them. This is your path to your wholeness." - Sev Joy

THE PATH TO FULFILLMENT

I was searching for meaning for so many years. I wanted to feel love, I wanted to feel me, but there was always something missing and holding on. This is how this flow started to rise; it was strange , uncomfortable, sometimes scary, until it became step by step my new identity, which I chose to embrace proudly in silence .

Being just in flow with my heart's desires makes me feel so alive. Open to receive all this abundance that life constantly offers me in different ways. So, I realized, I don't need any more approval, nor to compare myself. I just feel at peace with who I am. I feel it's within me with all my imperfection. It's just there, ready to be felt, ready to be seen.

I feel safe to express my voice freely, to be seen in all my colors, without any mask. There is a power of worth, the purity of self-love. There is a magic of standing for something more for myself without paying attention to what others will think anymore, without constantly doubting whether I am good enough.

This bravery of stepping into my truest version of me is a daily becoming. I simply choose to feed it every day, because love is like a flower; you have to take care of her daily; you have to provide all the nourishment she needs to help her grow within, so she can glow and expand her presence without pushing, just by being in her core.

Until today, experiencing all these lessons , I realized that everything is already there within us. You don't have to look outside, just listen to your inner voice.

Listen to your body's expression, listen to your emotions, be present to each of them, and feel free to express your uniqueness. You already have everything within; no one can give it to you better than you can. Sometimes, we just forget it when we are looking outside, comparing ourselves, and doubting. This is part of this journey, so be kind to yourself.

Celebrate yourself without specific reasons today; there is just this present moment that truly matters .You never know how many tomorrows you will have the opportunity to experience again.

> *"You always know it's the right thing when in the end*
> *there is peace." - Oprah Winfrey*

Letter to Myself!

This is the beauty of another priceless moment, taking time with myself and nourish my soul, and just let it be. Reflecting on it, I had finally realized that the love I had been looking for so long outside was just there sparkling within me, was just waiting to be discovered by myself step by step. Looking at this warrior's part of me, who continues to move forward, despite the fears and doubts. A fragile and strong woman, a princess who wants more than anything to share her love for life and her passion in this great human adventure. Let me publish this letter I wrote to myself a year ago...

"Dear Sev,

I feel so blessed I had this courage to open my eyes and to see how priceless you are. I discovered an amazing, courageous soul, passionate and aware of the beauty of world around her. One who has failed several times, but always got back on her feet. One who, in her simplicity, spreads joy around her. One who understood that sadness and grief are part of life's cycles. One who is afraid sometimes and who, despite everything, moves towards her dreams. One who does not accept mediocrity and continues on her path towards human fulfilment. One who regularly comes out of her comfort zone to move to the next step. One who knows more than anyone today that her life mission is to serve humanity with her gift of love and compassion and to leave a legacy to her children, for all children of tomorrow. This is you, Sev. Yes, you, darling. This smiling, caring, courageous, ambitious, intuitive woman. Never again beat yourself up for not knowing, because you already know that everything changes constantly and comes in the perfect moment. Never again compare yourself to others—you are unique and gifted exactly the way you are. You are enough; you are a beautiful soul.

I honor your choices of living in your truth and just embracing your authentic self, your best you, with all parts of you , even more than yesterday. I am so grateful to say today how proud I am to see who you have become since you were born. Thank you, Sev, for always being there for me; you never gave up on me, even in the darkest moments of my life. You took care of me, you protected me, and you had the courage to move forward, despite the storms and thunder. You always wanted the best for me. You're my best friend, my sweet star. Thank you for keeping inside me this eternal little courageous girl who appreciate the magic of life. Thank you for loving me as I am today. I still have so much to learn and to discover, and I know you will always be the *one the only one until the last day... I'm sorry, please forgive me, I love you, thank you."*

As I write these few words, it's like a revelation; I had not thought of publishing this letter in the middle of this book, but my heart guided me once again: this is exactly where it belongs. What I learned is that the most beautiful love story begins by loving oneself. Appreciating myself the way I am is essential to becoming fulfilled and filling my heart with joy every day. It is pure pleasure to share this *joie de vivre* around you when you feel good about yourself. You can only give the best of you when your heart is free.

I'm sharing with you this intense moment, because I'm sure that you, too, like me, sometimes forget to thank the most important person on this earth: you. Your presence has meaning, and each of us has a mission to accomplish, and we only can accomplish this mission at the fullest when we open our hearts, when we become aware of our greatness . It's up to you to find yours. It took me time to find my own. You don't have to waste your priceless time to find yours. Live it, give it, share it.

Sometimes, you just need to wake up and connect with your deepest dreams, allowing yourself to feel those feelings deeper, creating that space to receive what you want and deserve, even if it's not yet manifested in a physical way. You just feel like it's already done; you start to create that vibration with your desire, and then, you connect that message with your physical body, giving this opportunity to appreciate that feeling within.

But you need courage. Be real with who you are; don't be ashamed of expressing your truth, because it's yours, it's your authentic you, even if you will unintentionally create some pain to others. It's okay—

pain is part of life suffering; it's a choice . If it comes from this place of unconditional love and respect, they will feel it.

Be compassionate, feel love and give love... everybody, no matter where they are in their own journey, they deserve love and being loved just for who they are .

But first, you need start loving yourself for your choices, for just who you are. Start loving your weaknesses, not lying yourself and others. Allow yourself to feel you are different. BE YOU, express your voice— it will free your soul to live your purpose.

Sometimes, it's hard to find this balance within you; you think you don't know what's true between your vibration (your heart) and your beliefs (your head). You have doubts about yourself and your decision, you fight in silence, and so, you think you are not good enough.

So, you resist and continue to feel that conflict which is holding you back, and you avoid stepping into that conflict, because it's painful, so you start to procrastinate, you start to find pleasure in everything, just to avoid your pain... That's suffering, and when you suffer, you can't attract what you truly desire. You are disconnected; you are in survival instinct. You can't truly give your light with this inner conflict .

Remember: your gift is to shine with your presence , your authentic spark of your soul, your joy and appreciation of who you are. So, dare to take that first courageous step, this tiny step of self-love, by being kind to yourself and accepting you the way you are. Every day is just a new beginning. You are not your thoughts. Give yourself this permission to express your truth. Remember: it's just a journey. Journey back home.

So, feel what you want create in your own reality, and live it on a daily basis, and feel it, instead of focusing more on your fears of what's missing. Fears is also energy, so what you ask for is always given to you. That's part of your vibration, that part of your reality. So, wake up before it's too late; it's time to love who you are with all your heart.

It's okay to be vulnerable; just start the process... everything is going to be okay.

Thank you. I am forever so grateful for this love and abundance of life I receive every single day. Each connection in this world with each human being teaches me something special, something unique about myself and about my purpose.

This long path of healing my heart of suffering, of shame, of not being good enough, and of struggling of my childhood gave me this incredible power to open my heart and shine my light to the world. Day after day, I am so grateful I can expand my love to this entire world. By starting to allow myself to let go of all these fears and all my own judgement has opened my heart to vibrate at a level I have never felt before.

I am in peace now and feel this calmness inside of me, this safe place in my heart...

I am just a human being, and it's okay sometimes to have fear again and have some pain, but I don't have any more time to spend in suffering. I am just there for one moment. I am not perfect. I still make mistakes, but I just try my best every single day.

This habit of cultivating my daily gratitude gives me this oxygen of joy. Appreciation is my daily food, no matter what happens.

I decided definitely to just let it go and enjoy this priceless breath of my soul in each moment of my life. And in this level of vibration, I find my real purpose. Living my life with passion and appreciation.

This crystal clear vision and this unshakable faith give me access to touch with my open heart each human soul I cross in my way to help them do the same: free themselves to be free to love, to live with passion and purpose.

I am forever grateful for all the pain I received in my path. Without it, I would not be able today to understand and even more to feel all this process of healing and serving with love and compassion.

Instead of focusing on what's missing, it's time to spread more kindness and love to each others. Only love matters. All together, we can create this legacy. It's our responsibility to create impact, step by step, every single day, just by giving more love around us, forgiving more, and accepting more differences. We are the change we want to see in this world by becoming it and acting in that way.

Our kids need our example of courage, and it's our purpose to help them find this inner peace and confidence and create this new reality of planting these seeds of love. Let's show them by example by living it and sharing it today. Each story matters, each voice is a gift to all.

Life is beautiful. Just feel it today. We have another chance to express our unique voice of presence.

"Your light is seen. Your heart is known. Your soul is cherished by more people than you might imagine. If you knew how many others have been touched in wonderful ways by you, you would be astonished. If you knew how many people feel so much for you, you would be shocked. You are far more wonderful than you think you are. Rest with that. Rest easy with that. Breathe again. You are doing fine. More than fine. Better than fine. You're doing great. So relax. And love yourself today."

— Neale Donald Walsch

"I've learned that people will forget what you said, people will forget what you did, but people will never forget how you made them feel."

- Maya Angelou

How to Own my Presence:
Finding the Meaning in My Joy of Living

This journey with my ups and downs, with all my failures and victories, shows how everything goes fast. Life is just about moments, and the way we connect with each of this moments creates all the difference in how we feel and how we show up in life .It takes me time and courage to learn how to appreciate each part of this constant progress, this infinite learning about myself .

Something profound shifted in my way of connecting with the world when I started to connect deeper with myself.

So many different emotions gave me this opportunity to discover my treasure of having different feelings, being alive, and having the choice to live them fully and letting them go when they finished teaching me something about my own resistance.

I realized every time I resisted, it was an external sign of internal conflict .

I was pleasing others, avoiding connecting with my sadness, and trying to hide my frustration, my inner pain fully present to each emotion coming to me. I didn't realize I was controlling the way I felt. Being fully curious, I started to feel the impact of my own words, people's reactions around me, nature vibrations, and nature's power to calm my inner rush, the power of emotions and their different colors, my stories, and my own intentions and dreams!

I've had to learn to let things go, to free myself from this past story, from things that doesn't serve me anymore. I realized that my old patterns are what hurt me again and again, this emotional attachment to my old stories, which, of course, was this fear of not being good enough, not being worthy of love.

Being present to this moment with kindness and compassion and allowing myself to be fully opened to the unknown, courageously facing my fears in the middle of the darkness has become my new way of living my truth . I learned to observe, instead of react. Instead of trying to control or to fix it, I discovered step by step that everything is in alignment with just this present moment, and all my choices were just emotional reaction from what I knew from the past .Today I have a choice to change the way I look at life .

The most priceless lesson is freedom of all attachments and all expectation, which is really the essence of my spiritual path—being aware that I am free, that I belong to nothing and nothing belongs to me. Letting go of thoughts, patterns, people, things...just being in that moment free to receive each experience like a gift.

When you feel yourself present in that moment, you become free to love what it is, free to appreciate what life is offering you right now in this moment. You have no expectation, and in that moment, you feel peace and contentment. This is how you expand your presence and radiate light and love at the highest level.

When you let's go of any resistance, you feel like a bird. You fly and enjoy this unique moment you have to live now. You smile, or you just cry, or you just feel without questioning.

The only thing that creates separation between your beautiful state and suffering state is your attachment to your story you decided to believe, but your past doesn't exist anymore, only memories do. Living in the now, free from any expectation, allow yourself to be free and to just love what it is. Love this present moment, this specific challenge, and this present feeling. Be compassionate and move on . Your thoughts are just illusions. They aren't real until you keep believing that they are real by constantly thinking about them.

So, if you truly want to feel more peace to feel your heart's desire, clean your space from all old attachments that doesn't serve you anymore today, and focus on what will make you proud of you today. Each little tiny step you decide to make to feel happier and grateful for your life will bring you higher .

So, if you want more fulfillment in your daily life, more joy, more happiness, take time to do what makes your soul happy , and allow yourself to be grateful for what you have already . Life is always happening for us.

Focus your energy and time to create a new, vibrant space to receive this beautiful energy you want to attract in your reality today. Ask yourself this question: what's prevent you from feeling really happy now? What are you ready to let go of? What has to happen for you in order to feel joy or peace right now? Only what you focus on expands...

Sometimes, even if some sadness or anger arrive in my path, I don't try to hide those feelings anymore. I just learned to feel them consciously, take time to accept what it is, and explore this emotion to fully embrace the meaning behind that: this inner dance of each part of me allows me to express my heart more deeply, feeling more compassion for myself and for others, because they all do the best they could with what they have now.

I realized that joy is my religion, no matter what happens in my daily life, no matter how many challenges I meet in my way, because it will always happen. This is exactly the feeling I want to feel and enjoy for most of my lifetime: this inner peace, this playfulness and vulnerability, this courage of just being ME.

I'm feel so blessed for this feeling surrounded by so much love and intention of all the beautiful souls around the world, feeling this daily nature welcoming me every morning, enjoying my delicious food and water I have chance to have each day, enjoying my delicious chicory coffee each morning, having this opportunity to learn and share with others the secret of my authentic passion for life. Feeling this unconditional love of my family, my friends, my clients, and all of you who will read this book makes me feel so grateful, that just one story shared during my life journey could impact someone else's life. Feeling this grace in my daily life helped me open my heart to receive what life decides to offer me today. Becoming aware of this inner state of being is life-changing. How beautiful is just owning my greatness and being able to share that vulnerable me and most authentic gift of my love with others.

How beautiful is just being aware how our own transformation brings this light to life. All this journey of just being a little better version of myself every single day becomes my own form of resilience, my real success in life.

My intention here is helping you find your own way to express your gift of courage in this world by stepping into your power of your presence and to connect with your own source of joy.

Your presence matters and only you have the power to impact the world with your authentic story.

Living an awakening life may not be easy every day. It brings you to dance this unique song that only you have this capacity to hear deeply . And I know sometimes, you will dance alone. This chaos of life, you are afraid, but you continue to dance, and you follow your song, no matter what. And in that moment, magic happens.

Your song starts vibrating within your heart, with your truth... so you start losing yourself, your old self. When you let it go of who you thought you were, you open yourself to this new way of being, this radiant, authentic source of magnetic beauty . Yes, darling, the power resides inside of you. We all are in the same journey. I was there for a long time of my life, I felt lost, afraid, and guilty.

I realized that I am here to heal, just by being ME, and offering my heart of service to the greater good.

Magic happens when you start believing in magic. When you are no longer afraid of feeling some fear. When you just start expressing with courage and authenticity what you truly desire to feel on a daily basis. When you connect your heart with this moment, this unique present moment of your unique life.

You are here to explore and appreciate each chapter of your life journey. Only here in this moment resides the beauty of your own presence. Don't be afraid to shine your light: you have so much to give from this place of love and compassion for yourself.

You are here for a purpose, to heal your soul and to shine, and to help others do the same. This is your legacy.

And because of this beautiful journey, I found my purpose.

To be daily aware of this gift I have to breathe again, to appreciate each and every moment, to be able to be my best each and every day, and to make a difference in someone else's life. I can show up for women who are struggling with their own fears.

Today, I help other women own their presence by find their voice: by helping them love themselves for who they truly are, by letting go of what doesn't serve them anymore, guiding them to find their own purpose by connecting their heart to their deepest desires, connecting their body temple to the movement of joyful life, to live the life they deserve and truly enjoy the journey.

We are all in our own path, and want to become our greatest version, so it's exciting to start this journey with a first step at time. It's never too late. Just one little step in the direction of your dreams will make you feel alive today . What is yours?

Never give up your dreams, just find your why, have faith, be patient, and trust the process… you are here for reason.

> *"Not what we have but what we enjoy,*
> *constitutes our abundance."*
>
> *Epicurus*

What lights you up more than anything else in your life? Listen to whatever immediately comes to you – these are signs leading you to your true passion, your most heartfelt desire, and, ultimately, your destiny.

A FINAL WORD...

Nothing is more glorifying than the new person you become every single day. Every step—however small it may be—brings you closer to yourself and gives you access to an infinite way of new opportunities. Today, I am just saying thank you for each lesson received in my life, thank you for every challenge I've met. We are all creators of our own stories. We all live through happy and sad events in our lives. This colorful mix of unique experiences is our life story, and it is our most priceless gift we have to offer to this world. We have the power to change the script at any time; it's just about one decision, one courageous action. The most important thing is to find what truly matters to you during your time here, on Earth. What's your life purpose? How do you want to impact this world with your unique presence, adding value by your authentic, heartfelt contribution? What do you really want to live, feel, give, and share? Who do you want to become?

What does the joy of living mean to you ? How does it look? What has to happen to feel that inner joy now? Ask yourself these questions just once a day. I'm sure you have the answer inside your heart right now.

With Love

Be grateful for your life today. You have only a limited time to express your true potential, to express your love and your support to someone, to make a little difference by just one call, one smile, one great intention, one courageous step ...

Just be you.

Your presence is worth more than you think.

There is no space for resentment, judgment, nor envy—they are a waste of time and energy!!!

Let it go, forgive, and be present to what truly matters.

Make your day so special, because

YOU ARE A GIFT, and it all starts with you now.

COME BACK TO L.O.V.E
AND STAY THERE

I would love to share with you a simple way to quickly turn your fear into love any time when fear comes back: this will be the only four steps that can immediately bring you back home, back to LOVE and living the life you deserve.

We all experience some fear in each season in our life: fear of not being good enough, fear of not being loved, fear of rejection, fear of failure, fear of death, fear of what others will say if... This feeling is human, and the good news we are not alone—we are all in the same boat. But there is a big difference between being used by fear or using fear to move forward to love, to that place of peaceful feeling, to gratitude.

It's time for a new chapter in your life where being that presence of love will be your daily pleasure. Where joy and gratitude will be your daily seeds of nourishment

Tomorrow is not granted .You only have this lifetime to feel fully alive to share your love and to be that source of peace by living it daily within.

Those four steps of L.O.V.E. helped me transform my daily connection with life, itself, and transform all relationships around me and the most important relationship: the one I have with myself. You can use it and transform your quality of life and fully embrace who you are at your core each day of the rest of your precious life without wasting your energy on things that don't bring you joy or inner satisfaction.

L - Listen to your heart.

Your inner voice already knows your calling. You are born to be happy to fulfill your destiny every single day you are guided, and only you have this power to turn your dreams into a reality or not. This inner voice is the essence of your being the place of all healing. This guidance always shows you the right way. Sometimes, it is not the one you expected. So, any time you have a doubt and this fear arises, it's because it comes from your thoughts, your memories, which are created in your head to protect you, to make you feel safe. From the scientific perspective, it is proven that the brain doesn't see the difference between real experience or the one you imagined.

To allow yourself to listen to this inner truth, you need to come back to your heart, to your body, to this stillness of your being. Any time you feel this doubt and fear arise ,put your hand on your heart take seven deep breaths and just listen to it; you don't have to rush, just surrender and let it be just the way it is. Be present with each breath.

Ask yourself these questions:

1. What does this fear try to teach me at this specific moment ?

2. Where is this energy of fear located in my body ? Take seven deep breaths into that space and just observe this feeling. Just be one with it. Be grateful for this feeling. It's just a feeling; just let it be. Remember, everything is going to be okay; you are safe.

3. Is that fear real, or is it just a consequence of my actual thoughts?

4. If this thought didn't exist, how would I love to feel instead ?

5. What has to happen for me to feel this desired state now?

Take a seven deep breaths again. Feel this beating of your heart, and remember a moment when you truly feel that feeling of peace, love, harmony, courage, and appreciation. Just pick one and feel it. Close your eyes and feel it deeply... What is the color of this feeling? What is the smell of it? How does it make you feel right now?

6. What is the truth? What you have to remember?

The more you will listen to this inner little voice and nurture yourself from within, spending more time in the present moment, in silence, the more your life begins to flourish. Only in that space of complete presence is where magic happens! Listening to your heart is just aligning yourself with the flow of your heart frequency. When something seems not aligned with your core, you will immediately feel it, and there will be no more resistance, because it's not your vibration. So, allow yourself to come back regularly to the silence, and just listen carefully.

Listening to your heart gives you access to this infinite power, this place where everything starts. All your dreams only become a reality if you allow yourself to take uncomfortable action, and be patient and kind with yourself.

Remember: fear will always come back in your life experience the moment you expect the least. We can't control outside events; they will happen for sure. This is part of this life journey, itself. But only you have the power to take control of how you feel by choosing the way you look at each experience.

O - Open your heart to be in present moment.

When you open your heart to be in the present moment, a new possibility starts to show up in your life. It's a place where you can give a new meaning to each situation. Your open heart starts channeling this inner light, even if you don't really know what it is or which form it will bring. Trust the process, even if you have to walk alone for a while.

Don't beat yourself up because you don't yet see the results you wanted. Instead, appreciate your becoming, your journey of learning, your courage in each little step of progress. Where there is progress, there is a natural part of the unknown, so there is a natural part of fear. So, open yourself to look at that fear differently. See and feel her like an energy to help you move to beyond.

When you open yourself to be fully present to this moment, you see life from a different perspective; you allow yourself to express your feelings more freely, because there's just this moment.

Only feelings not expressed create this inner resistance, which maintains this level of fear and produces hurting and destructive emotions in your whole body. There is not only one way to grow .There are always different ways of bringing you to your destination, to your home sweet home, your fulfilled presence. Maybe you can learn something from this new way of looking at this specific situation. Maybe this courage to open yourself helped you go out of your comfort zone and embrace the change you needed to become your best by using your hidden resources you have within.

By opening yourself, your resilience grows and finally allows you to let go of what doesn't serve you anymore. It's become your effortless place of letting go of control.

Only from this open space, you will be ready to forgive fully, because you have nothing to resist anymore. It will come naturally. You will feel it in each part of your being. Your openness will allow you to feel others, just like you are in their own journey of becoming. People who don't deserve your energy will naturally disappear in your life, and you will be able to feel which energy is lifting you up.

Openness is a place of no resistance to change, because everything constantly changes, even your emotions. It's a place of curiosity and hunger for growth. It's a place of total uncertainty that you consciously choose to embrace with no expectation anymore.

When you allow yourself to be present in that moment, just the way you are free of any thoughts or judgements, ready to receive life's gifts, there is the beginning of your treasure; there is where your presence starts to expand. You crave for more of this aliveness .This is how you have this courage to express this next step of your uniqueness : your vulnerability.

V - VULNERABILITY sets you free.

It's a step where you have courage to jump in your darkest parts and embrace them fully: your vulnerability will open the doors to the bravest part of your soul. The part you have hidden for so long . This step will allow you courageously to show up for yourself. There is a stage where you don't care anymore what others think; it's just your unique truth. You are not afraid to be seen for who you truly are. Your heart is in flow, expressing its truth without holding any mask, without lying to yourself anymore. This is a place where the first time you courageously embrace your scars: your shame, anger, resentment, your own judgement of not feeling worthy, not good enough. This a place of deep healing. Expressing your vulnerability is truly loving yourself fully. It's being honest with yourself and others.

The first time you show the world that you are just a human being who is imperfectly beautiful, the right people will resonate with the depths of your authenticity; they will feel you. Your story, your courage will resonate with their own story. They will feel love and respect for you, and your vulnerability becomes a source of inspiration for them. You will see that you are not alone, and even more, you can help them. There is no place of pleasing anymore, but standing for who you truly are, raising your standard with all respect and love for your being.

This is a place where you recognize the value of your worth. No one can give it; only you can. This place of vulnerability allows you to set your new boundaries that align with your higher vision for yourself. The beauty of your imperfection becomes your greatest gift to offer to yourself, and the world will benefit from this healing.

So, ask yourself: which part of your darkness did you hide for so long, beating yourself up and hurting yourself and others by not living your truth?

Which part of your scars are you still holding deep in your heart and avoiding sharing with yourself?

Only the truth can set you free; only from that place you can truly jump into that place of pure joy and appreciation of being YOU; your best you each and every day.

This is how you jump into that fourth step of your expansion .

E- Expansion of your presence to the world.

Your presence is the most precious gift you have to offer to this world. When you become aware that only from that place of harmony and peaceful presence within, there is no place for fear, only expansion of love . Expansion of greatness and kindness, which is your natural state of being in this life experience.

In that place of flow, there is peace, the warmth of joyful feeling expressed freely everywhere from your being. There is just a field of divine light, a source of all miracles , a place of all healing , a place of blissful living in the now. There is a place of gratitude for everything that life is abundantly giving you freely.

There is no comparison , no judgement , no resentment; there is just a place of worth and deep compassion .There's just this inner knowing, this feeling of contentment.

Your expression of peace and love in your own being reflects this wave of peace on others. It's a ripple effect around you, in your family, your community, and even larger, in the world . Remember: we are just energy in this human body. The vibration of your unique energy you put to the world is the vibration you always receive back . That is why each intention, each thought, each word is just an expression of who you are. So, choose wisely which energy you would love to spend the most of your time.

Any time you doubt yourself or you feel that fear within rising again, just remember you are doing your best, you are always guided, and everything is going to be okay.

Fear is not who you are. You always have a choice, and the only thing that prevents you from moving forward is just your scared mind and your stories you repeat continually to protect yourself.

Fear is just an illusion; it's just an energy you can use to move you in the direction of your dreams .So, use it wisely.

This precious path to fulfillment , this wholeness of your being, is an art of dancing between both fear and love. Be aware that you and only you have control of the way you feel. So, it's never too late to start listening to your heart's desires and choose a new direction by intentionally using the energy of fear in service to greater good to LOVE, to your highest purpose.

This is my gift to each of you. Just feel it, embrace it.

> "The power of love is here now
> The power of now is here now
> The power of you and me is here
> To create magic on earth
>
> Let the water wash away your tears
> Let the fire burn away your fears
> Let the wind blow into your life such faith and trust
> Let the earth hold you, take care of you, and nurture you."

Alexia Chellun

Let it be your blessing today, this moment of honoring and nourishing yourself. Your life is precious; celebrate it today .Make a self-love your priority. Remember: you are beautiful just the way you are, and you can achieve anything you desire. It's up to you to make your dream a reality.

The only beauty you can see is with your own eyes. Everything starts there . Your perception of the world around you will completely change the day when you can deeply feel that worth, this pure treasure within.

When I started writing this book, I put this intention to my heart and promised myself that this book would support children's education in need, children in orphanages, abused kids , sexually abused kids, families who still crave for food every day, and helping abused women to find their beauty within .

So, part of this book's earnings will be given to support what is most important to our future generation, bringing hope and love by supporting those who need the most!

I have supported my little orphanage window of life in Masindi, Uganda for five years now, and I have been so blessed that I have been able to give my best to change the lives of 23 children already. Don't be afraid to start small. Start believing in yourself, and see magic happen.

JOY is my religion, LOVE is my LEGACY.

With love 🖤

Sev Joy

ACKNOWLEDGEMENTS

This book exists today thanks to the encouragement and support I received from many people throughout my life. I thank all the people in my life and in particular:

A huge thank you to my beloved brother, Jacek. Thanks to you, my mission in life has meaning. You are my inspiration, my light source. Your love for life, your smile, and your courage is a daily invitation to happiness. You taught me to appreciate every moment as if it were the last. Continue to send this light around you—you are a source of good. I love you from the bottom of my heart.

I am so grateful that I crossed your way, Tony Robbins. You became my mentor, to whom I owe so much in this journey of self-discovery. Nineteen years ago, I found your book, *Awaken the Giant Within You*, at an airport. Everything happens at the right time and for a reason. You gave me access to an extraordinary source of energy that I had previously underestimated for so many years: the power of my heart. Your humble presence and this passion with which you impacted so many lives in this world resonate in my heart. Your soul is so pure and beautiful, and your heart so big. You guided me like you guided all these brothers and sisters on this journey back home, and since then, my dreams have continued to grow. I found the courage to live my truth. You are such a blessing to this world. Thank you.

Thank you to my husband, Anthony, without whom this journey would not have been the same. It's a gift to share one part of our life together and experience each up and down of this journey . You have been there for me. I admire your courage and determination. Living beside you has made me understand that our differences are the most precious gift of life, to help me grow and understand what makes a relationship works. Our differences have helped us challenge ourselves and magnify this unconditional love that unites us. Everything that comes our way is a gift. Thank you for the beautiful soul you are. It's in this darkest moment in our life together, I learned so much about myself and all resistance holding me back to express my deepest appreciation just for who you are as a human being. You have always done your best. Thank you for that. I not always seen things that way, so please forgive me. I love you, and thank you.

I thank my children, Kelyan and Lea. You constantly open up my eyes on what is the most extraordinary thing: giving life. You are my most beautiful mission, you are my teachers. You must know that all your dreams will become reality if you deeply desire them. If your dreams help humanity, all the energy of the Universe will be aligned to realize this masterpiece—your masterpiece. Because a dream can change a person's destiny, a family's destiny, or a community's destiny. So, dream big, my darlings, and keep your children's hearts for the rest of your lives.

Dear Aunt Krystyna, you've always been my guardian angel; you are my sun. The door to your heart was always open to me, as if I had been your own daughter. You helped me with my homework, and you took the time to listen to me. It is an honor for me to have had a woman like you in my life. Thank you for all this motherly love and all this generosity you gave to all my family. Your presence in my life is a gift. I honor you, and I love you forever.

Dear Mariusz, my brother, thank you. You were always there for Jacek and me. It is an honor to have known someone like you, who has helped so many children, from Poland to Uganda. With your humanitarian actions, you are a brother of humanity. You are a beautiful force for good; you're an inspiration to so many people. With your big heart, your simplicity, and your discretion, you changed many lives. I am proud to have crossed your path. You'll always have a place in my heart. Thanks to you and your family, contributing has become a natural part of my life. Thank you.

Thank you to my sister-in-law, Kasia Czaja, for always being at my side in difficult times. You've always reached out; you're like a sister to me. Thank you for taking care of my brother. I honor you for that, and thank you very much for always believing in me.

I also want to express my deepest respect and gratitude to Sage Robbins. First of all, thank you for the wonderful woman that you are, for your support and your unconditional love to your husband. Through your presence, your purity, and your inner content joy, you heal so many souls in this world. Your simplicity and your feminine energy particularly touched my heart. Thank you for this priceless connection and blessings I have been so blessed to receive. *Namaste.*

Thank you to those special souls who had such a special place in my heart in my journey: Kate Boyer, Michelle Madrid Branch, Dawn Watson, Chris Weaver, Marvin, Johanne, Sondra, Angie, Julie, and Jan.

A special thank you to my publisher, Michael Butler, who trusted in my story, and was so patient with my process of creation.

I probably forgot some special people, so please receive all my love and thanks for being part of my life experience.

Sincerely.

"When you make loving others the story of your life, there is never a final chapter because the legacy continues. You lend your light to one person, and he or she shines it on another and another and another. "

Oprah Winfrey